Senior Moments

Senior Moments

S. L. Varnado

iUniverse, Inc.
New York Lincoln Shanghai

Senior Moments

iUniverse books may be ordered through booksellers or by contacting:

iUniverse
2021 Pine Lake Road, Suite 100
Lincoln, NE 68512
www.iuniverse.com
1-800-Authors (1-800-288-4677)

ISBN-13: 978-0-595-39688-7 (pbk)
ISBN-13: 978-0-595-84094-6 (ebk)
ISBN-10: 0-595-39688-7 (pbk)
ISBN-10: 0-595-84094-9 (ebk)

Printed in the United States of America

To my son Larry, without whose technical help this book would never seen the light of day
And to my wife Mary Lou, who patiently listened to these little sketches as they were written.

Contents

Introduction

The following essays were begun as a series of Letters to the Editor in the Mobile Press Register, a daily newspaper published in Mobile, Alabama. They were supposed to be humorous—but whether they were or not is a matter of opinion. I wrote dozens of them—every day a new letter. The staff of the newspaper was going mad. "How can we stop this man?" they asked. At last, Mr. Michael Marshall, the editor of the paper, called me on the phone. "Mr. Varnado, instead of writing all those letters, would you like to write a regular monthly column for us?" (I suspect this was Mr. Marshall's way of rendering me harmless—"kicking me upstairs" so to speak.). I considered the matter carefully and two seconds later agreed.

The column has gone on now for about three years—with mixed results. My wife, family and friends say it is occasionally funny. My enemies maintain an uncomfortable silence. The vast majority of readers ignore the thing completely. But I am not discouraged. Writing humor is a dangerous job. Look at the great humorists of the past: Aristophanes, Swift, Twain, Voltaire—all dead. The job must be dangerous!

A friend who I met in the grocery store one day, and whose name I could not remember at the moment, suggested the title of the column to me. "So?" he said. "Having a senior moment, are you?" That was the first time I had heard the phrase, and I fell in love with it. It sounds so much more refined than saying, "Getting senile, are you?"

Most of the essays in this book are based upon real, if slightly exaggerated, experiences. Some are pure fantasy. My intention was to divert the reader from the troubles and tribulations of life by producing a smile—or even a laugh.

A word about my picture. "Looks like the Phantom of the Opera," a friend remarked. The truth is: photographs do not bring out the best in me. I am not handsome, but I think a good portrait painter could improve on my looks. Of course, I would want the portrait to be realistic. Remember Oliver Cromwell's words to his portrait painter: "Paint me warts and all." I suppose he planned to give the portrait to his mother-in-law.

Is the Alternative Really Worse?

Like many retired couples, my wife and I spend a lot of our time seeing doctors. We see urologists, neurologists, cardiologists, dentists and the man our HMO refers to as our Primary Physician. (I suppose they call him "primary" because he's the first step on the road to trouble.) Keeping up with our appointments gets complicated, so to avoid confusion we have a large calendar hanging in the kitchen with our appointments clearly listed.

Recently, the calendar said it was time for my visit to the urologist. I had only been to him once before, but thought I remembered where his office was. I arrived promptly at eight thirty, signed in and had the usual two-hour wait. I worked a crossword puzzle, read a 1989 copy of the *American Electrician's Journal* and finally drifted off to sleep.

When I awoke, a nurse was calling my name, and the other patients were smiling behind their magazines. With some embarrassment, I followed the nurse into one of those bare, depressing little cells where doctors always confine you before they see you. I suppose these rooms are intended to break your spirit—doctors like their patients humble. The room contained nothing except an examining table, an assortment of surgical knives, and a brightly colored chart of the nervous system. The man pictured on the chart had a round expressionless face. He looked as if he had lost all interest in life—and who could blame him? A day or two in that little cell would depress anybody.

An hour later, the doctor came bustling in, clipboard in hand. "Good morning. I'm Dr. Carberry, filling in for Dr. Brunswitch." He glanced at his clipboard. "Now let me see—you are Mr. Varnado, right?" I nodded. He studied the clipboard with a rather troubled expression. The silence grew unbearable. To ease the tension, I said: "So how do the old kidneys look, doc?"

He gave me a blank stare. "Kidneys? Is something wrong with our kidneys?"

"You tell me, doc. You're the urologist."

"Urologist? But I'm not a urologist. I'm a neurologist."

I turned red with embarrassment. "Gosh, doc. I'm afraid I've made a bad mistake. May I use your phone?"

He looked annoyed. "I suppose so."

I dialed the office of my urologist. "Good morning," I told the clerk. "This is Mr. Varnado. I had an appointment with the doctor this morning, but I'm afraid I missed it."

There was a brief pause. "I'm looking through our list of morning appointments, and I don't see your name, Mr. Varnado."

"Must be some mistake. Sorry to have bothered you." With a growing sense of confusion, I hung up. Maybe the appointment was with my Primary Physician. I dialed his number and got one of his clerks, who put me on "hold." Ten minutes later, a voice said: "Who are you holding for?"

"A clerk put me on hold. I wanted her to check and see if I have an appointment with the doctor. My name is Varnado."

"Is that Mr. or Mrs. Varnado?"

I exerted admirable restraint. "It's Mr. Varnado," I said politely.

"I see no listing for a Mr. Varnado. Is this an emergency?"

"Not that I'm aware of."

"Well, Mr. Varnado, I see no appointment for you this morning. Unless this is an emergency…"

"I've already told you that it's not an emergency."

"Then why are you calling?"

"Because I enjoy bothering people," I said, hanging up the phone.

I dialed home. When my wife answered, I said: "Go look at our calendar and see if I have a doctor's appointment this morning?"

She returned a few moments later. "The calendar says 'Urologist.'"

"The calendar is wrong!"

"You sound agitated. Why don't you come home and take a nice nap?"

I did just that, but it didn't help. I had a nightmare in which Dr. Josef Mengele was operating on me. I awoke with the phone ringing. "Hello,

Mr. Varnado. This is your urologist's office calling to remind you that you have an appointment with us at three o'clock. Please be on time."

I'm thinking of giving up doctors altogether. Dying would be less complicated.

It Does Not Compute

I am forced to admit that I am too old for many of today's inventions. I cannot successfully operate a VCR. Mobile phones rattle me. I have to get one of my grandchildren to show me how to open a childproof bottle of aspirin. All this should have been a warning to me: don't buy a computer.

Nevertheless, I bought one. The purchase was entirely due to the herd instinct. Most of my friends have computers. My grandchildren can operate them. What finally convinced me, however, was the day my garbage man told me he uses a computer to arrange his pick-up schedule.

I entered the computer store hesitantly. The smiling clerk sized me up immediately. "Thinking about buying a computer, but figure you're too old to learn, eh," he said. "No problem. Recently I sold one to a 98-year-old grandmother, and she's already a whiz at it. You'll master the thing in half an hour." Was the man a liar? I don't know. I would only suggest that he should seriously consider a career in politics!

I bought the thing, and when it arrived, my son (who understands these matters) put it together in my study. In place of my trusty old manual typewriter, my antique powder horn and my other keepsakes, there was now a mass of wires and machinery that made my comfortable study look like Dr. Frankenstein's laboratory.

"To start the computer, press this button," my son urged. I pressed the button. The machine blinked, burped and the screen lit up. A curious display of tiny pictures appeared. They looked like miniature paintings by Salvador Dali: a notebook with wings, a globe with an arrow through it, a badly drawn ice tray and other oddities. "What are those strange pictures?" I asked.

"They're called icons," my son replied.

"I thought icons were found in Greek Orthodox Churches."

"Don't try to be funny," he said impatiently. (I was not trying to be.) "Now click the icon that says 'Word Perfect.'" I obeyed. A small, white box mysteriously appeared in one corner of the monitor. It said: "Open, File, Save For Web Page, Send to Recycle Bin." None of these sounded particularly enticing to me.

"Hit the one that says, 'Open,'" my son told me. When I did, the computer made a burping noise, and a blank screen appeared. "Now type something," my son urged.

"What shall I type?"

"Anything. How about the Gettysburg Address?"

I tried to type the opening words of the speech: "Four score and seven years ago." What came out, however, was: "Poor gore and seven beers ago."

"Dad, you're pressing too hard on the keys. This isn't your old manual typewriter. It's sensitive—delicate. Imagine yourself gently stroking a butterfly."

So I tried to imagine myself gently stroking a butterfly. It must have been a rather psychotic butterfly, however. The monitor read: "four whores and heaven fears a bore."

My son was getting impatient. He handed me the instruction manual. "Read this!" he said and went into the kitchen to get a cup of coffee.

I felt like a man abandoned on a desert island. My hands were shaking. I glanced through the manual. It was written in several different languages, including Danish. I read the English section: "The following illustration shows the micro-tower, the mid tower, the front panel, the keyboard and the hard drive. Be sure you understand these units before continuing." This—to a man who can't open a childproof bottle of aspirin. The Danish version would have been more help.

I decided to experiment. After chasing the tricky little arrow up and down the screen for a while, I managed to position it on the icon that resembled an ice tray. I clicked, and a blank screen appeared. I clicked again. A smaller screen appeared inside the first one. I kept on clicking until there was a whole series of screens, each one inside its predecessor, like a maze of mirrors in a Glass House at the fair.

I grew desperate. I continued to click and the screens continued to multiply. I was in trouble. I yelled for my son. He slouched back into the room, sipping a cup of coffee and looking annoyed. "What now?" he asked.

"I don't like this thing, and it doesn't like me. I want my old manual typewriter back. And a bottle of aspirin—not the kind with a childproof cap!"

"Be patient," he said. "Stick with it. You'll learn."

That was a week ago. I haven't learned. In fact, I've gotten worse. I work on the thing for hours each day. I've lost all track of time. My eyes are slits. My wife is threatening to divorce me.

I suggest that computers, like cigarettes, should carry a warning label: "The Surgeon General has determined that computers may be dangerous to the sanity of anyone over the age of 65." This would prevent a lot of psychiatrist bills—and suicides.

Matches Made in Heaven

Why must colors always match? Why can't you wear a chartreuse shirt, purple slacks, red polka dot tie, and blue sandals? Or an orange vest, lavender suspenders and a yellow hat? I never worry about such matters—but my wife does. She's a fanatic about colors. Everything must match. The pink flowers in the carpet must "pick up" the rose color in the drapes. Her orange purse must match her yellow dress. And so on, *ad nauseam*.

"You're a mess," she often tells me. "That outfit you're wearing looks like something designed by Dr. Seuss."

"So what? Nature doesn't always match. Look at the rainbow: all seven colors splashed together in profusion."

"If I had wanted a rainbow, I'd have married one," she replies. "Look at you: Your socks don't match. You're wearing a green sock and a pink one."

"So? I like a little variety in my haberdashery."

This kind of argument usually starts when we're getting ready to attend a party or other social event. I pace up and down our bedroom while my wife puts the finishing touches on her make-up.

The bathroom door flies open. She emerges, clad in a blue silk dress and carrying a yellow purse. There is a hysterical look in her eyes.

"Finally ready?" I ask, glancing impatiently at my watch.

"Almost," she says, "but first I have to change purses. This yellow one doesn't match my dress." She runs to the closet and digs through a mountain of purses.

"Better hurry," I suggest, jingling the car keys. "We'll be late for the party."

"I *am* hurrying," she replies with an edge to her voice. "Go warm up the car."

"I've explained a dozen times that modern cars don't need warming up."

"Well, change the oil. Check the air in the tires. Do *something*."

Bearing several purses in her hands, she rushes to the bed, holds up the yellow purse and shakes it vigorously—much like a garbage man shaking a garbage can. Out come lipstick tubes, nail polish, eyebrow tweezers, grocery store receipts, rubber bands, pencil stubs, credit cards, band-aids—and I know not what. With a deft motion, she sweeps these objects into a blue purse, zips it closed and says, "I'm ready!"

"I'm delighted to hear it." I reply sarcastically, "but one question troubles me: does it really make much difference whether you carry a yellow purse or a blue one?"

"Of course it matters. It matters a lot. Every woman at the party would notice that my purse didn't match my dress. It's the way the female mind works."

"Then there's something radically wrong with the female mind. Suppose I took the same attitude? Suppose every time I changed my suit, I went through my wallet, removed credit cards, driver's license, etc., and put them in a wallet that matched the color of my suit? Wouldn't you think me a bit odd?"

"I already think you're a bit odd," she replies. Suddenly, she stops dramatically. "Wait. I've changed my mind. I think the maroon purse would look better." And she begins the process of changing purses again.

"This is ridiculous," I growl. "Will you ever be ready?"

"Of course! I'm ready now. Wait! These shoes don't match my dress."

"And people wonder why God put men in charge of things!"

In a flash, I realize I've gone too far. She's not a big feminist, but she has her limits. And I've just overstepped them.

Oh, well—at least I died with my unmatched socks on!

Challenging the Information Age

We live in The Information Age, but, despite all the new electronic gadgets in use these days, it's almost impossible to get information. For example:

My wife and I were planning to visit our son in Austin, Texas, and my wife suggested we go by Amtrak.

I dialed the 800 number. "Hello," said a mechanical voice "I'm Stella. Please answer my questions in a loud clear voice. To what city do you wish to travel?"

"Austin," I said in what I thought was a loud clear voice.

"Excuse me. Did I hear 'Boston?'"

"No, not Boston. Austin—in Texas."

"Excuse me. Did I hear 'Often in taxis?'"

"No, Austin, Texas. And we want to go by Amtrak."

"What day do you wish to travel?"

"Sunday!" I said loudly.

"Excuse me. Did I hear 'Someday?'"

"No," I replied. "Sunday."

"I'm sorry. I'm having trouble hearing you. May I switch you to a live agent?"

A few seconds later, a high-pitched voice came on the line. "Hello, Hello. My name Punjab Ramayana. I am speaking from Calcutta. Where you wish go, pliss?"

"I wish go Austin," I said. "My wife she wish go Austin too. We both wish go Austin."

"Excuse, pliss. You say 'Boston?'"

"No," I shouted. "I no say Boston. I say Austin. Austin, Texas."

"Taxes? So sorry! You have wrong number. This not tax bureau."

"I no want tax bureau! May I speakee with other agent."

"Yiss, yiss! Hold line please. I switch you to other agent."

After a pause, another voice came on the line. "Hello. Hello. This Mohammed Mustapha in Pakistan. Where you wish go, pliss?"

"Austin," I shouted.

"You say Boston?" Mohammed asked.

"No, I not say Boston. I say Austin...in Texas."

"You say 'Often in taxis?' Sorry! We not make taxi reservations."

I hung up the phone in despair.

"What's wrong?" the wife asked. "Why did you keep screaming 'Boston?'"

I paused for a moment. "Because I've always wanted to go to Boston. I love the place: its symphony orchestra...its baked beans...its historic buildings..."

"I think you're out of your mind," she said. "Go lie down and take an aspirin."

"Excuse, pliss. You say Aspen? That in Colorado, yis? I all time want go Aspin. Pliss pack suitcase and skis. We hitch-hike Aspin!"

Men vs. Women

Lawrence Summers, the president of Harvard University, made headlines recently by describing an experiment he conducted on his young daughter. He gave her two toy trucks to play with—and she immediately named one of them "Papa Truck" and the other "Baby Truck." Summers thought this proved that women were not as good at engineering and math as men.

These ivory tower types just can't be trusted. I wouldn't be surprised to learn that Summers is the kind of man who asks women their age and maybe even their weight. He's either crazy—or just tired of living.

Admittedly, there *are* differences between men and women—but the differences have nothing to do with intellectual ability. As an amateur psychologist (and a long time married man) I have compiled a list of some of the differences. See what you think:

1) Men and women show their feelings differently. When a man is happy, he smiles all over himself. If he had a tail he would wag it. Not so a woman. You can never be sure how a woman feels. She smiles when she's angry and cries when she's happy. If you ask her if she'd like to go to a movie, she says "No!"—And later complains that you never take her out.

2) Men love automobiles and their engines. Women also love automobiles—but could care less about what makes them run. A man is wasting his breath when he tells his wife the horsepower and torque of the car he just bought. All his wife wants to know is whether the color matches her new outfit.

3) When a man is tired he gets quiet. When a woman is tired, she likes to talk. A wise husband carries a tape recorder around with him and records bits of conversation during the day. That evening, he plays the tape while his wife cooks supper. She doesn't care—she just likes the noise.

4) Women are cleaner than men—but men are better organized than women. A clever husband lets the water run in the shower every night to

convince his wife he's taking a bath. A clever wife locks the door of the hall closet so her husband won't see the mess inside. This is not dishonesty—just diplomacy.

5) Women remember the dates of birthdays, anniversaries, etc. Men remember the dates of sporting events. These different abilities can be usefully merged. The wife says: "I hope you're not going to forget our anniversary this year." The husband replies: "How can I? It comes three days after the Super Bowl."

6) Women are sentimental and like to keep things. Men like to throw things away. A wife asks: "What ever happened to that valentine I gave you thirty years ago?" A wise husband quickly replies "I keep it in my safe deposit box at the bank." Little white lies never hurt anybody—except divorce court lawyers.

7) Finally—men are convinced of their own brilliance, but women need to be constantly told how smart they are. An experienced husband, for example, will say, "Honey, it was clever of you leave the car in the street last night. Sure, it got stolen—but I was going to trade it in anyway. Now the insurance will help pay for a new one." Such a husband can look forward to his Golden Wedding Anniversary.

These little differences make life interesting—and you don't need to be the president of Harvard to understand this simple truth!

Survival of the Unfittest

I am of two minds about the Theory of Evolution. When I go to the zoo and see an orangutan studying me with a deep and scholarly gaze, I am inclined to believe the theory. The orangutan looks brighter than some of the professors at the college where I teach. On the other hand, when I see a dog chasing its tail and barking idiotically, I have my doubts. Was this the way our early ancestors behaved? According to family lore, one of my ancestors chased women—but not his own tail.

Charles Darwin based his theory of evolution on what he termed "the survival of the fittest." I'm not sure what this means, but it sounds as if Darwin led a troubled life or had a difficult mother-in-law. Maybe his theory was the result of hard knocks!

At any rate, I enjoy puzzling over the theory and applying it to animals I have known. One of my favorite subjects for speculation is Big Boy, a gray alley cat that adopted us about ten years ago and has been hanging around our patio ever since. I'm sure that if Darwin had known Big Boy, he would have called his theory "the survival of the unfittest." Although the cat has survived to old age, he doesn't seem to be among the fittest of his species.

In the first place, he is the world's biggest coward. Despite his immense size, he is afraid of everything in the neighborhood. When I put his pan of food out each morning, he slinks hesitantly onto the patio, leaps up on the table and bolts the food down, glancing around suspiciously—like an Enron executive on the lookout for the F.B.I. He is, in fact, far too nervous to enjoy his food. I can't imagine why he hasn't died long ago of indigestion.

There is a small Siamese cat that sometimes comes up on the patio while Big Boy is eating. Big Boy (who is twice her size) runs away when she approaches, climbs a tree and watches her as she finishes his food.

When the Siamese leaves, Big Boy returns to the empty pan and nibbles at the crumbs. Like all forms of cowardice, it's a pitiful sight to behold. Obviously, he doesn't get much fun out of his meals.

Big Boy's worst nightmare, however, is a family of raccoons that sometimes visit our patio. When the mother raccoon appears, leading her troop of little raccoons, Big Boy hovers anxiously on the patio wall, gazing in fear as they eat his food. His fears are doubled when the father raccoon joins the group—Big Boy darts away like a UPS delivery truck that's running behind schedule.

He is afraid of dogs, possums, snakes, large turtles—and especially my grandchildren! When the grandchildren visit us, he disappears and stays gone for a week or more. When he finally returns, he displays no sense of shame. He's just glad they're gone.

He has absolutely no talent for hunting. Occasionally, he makes a half-hearted attempt to catch one of the many squirrels that play around our patio. He will sit poised for hours, tense as a rubber band, awaiting his chance to spring. When he *does* make his move, however, he invariably misses the squirrel. This never seems to bother him. He simply yawns and takes a nap. Once in a while, he catches a mole, which he then deposits on our back steps, mewing plaintively in his high voice. Apparently, he would like to be thought brave, but lacks the ambition to do anything about it. His instincts are those of a rabbit rather than those of his ancestor, the tiger.

But wait a minute! Maybe it is this very "unfitness" that accounts for his longevity. An old adage tells us that "discretion is the better part of valor." Likewise, the Bible says, "The race is not always to the swift, nor the battle to the strong."

Darwin might not agree, but I'm sure Big Boy would!

Mountains Out of Molehills

Moles are cute little creatures, but they can be big pests—like certain members of the feminine sex I have known. Given the proper environment, a mole can ruin a lawn quicker than you can make a 911 call to your Orkin man. I am told that they are blind; and I know for a fact that they are stupid. For no apparent cause or motive, they will tunnel up your lawn, leaving behind an embarrassing trail of mounds that look like the work of a miniature backhoe. Recently, one of them got a contract to excavate our front lawn. Since our lawn already looks like a Martian landscape, it didn't bother me much—but it bothered my wife.

"There's something strange going on in our front yard," she said as I lugged in the groceries from one of her shopping forays. "There are little mounds and ridges all over the place. Some of them look like tiny volcanoes."

"It's a mole," I told her. "I noticed him yesterday."

"How do you know it's a mole?" she asked suspiciously.

"Because I know moles," I said in an authoritative voice. "Didn't they have them in New York when you were growing up?"

"I suppose they did," she said, "but we never had any in our yard."

"Well," I said, "your knowledge has been sadly neglected. Do you want me to take care of him?"

"Yes," she murmured, "but don't hurt the poor thing. It may have a family."

Later that day, I dropped by our local hardware store and bought a can of mole poison. When I got home, I took a long handled spoon, dug some holes in the yard, and inserted several of the nasty looking little pellets. "That should do it," I muttered, dusting my hands off. "Any ole Southern boy knows how to get rid of moles."

That night as we were sitting down to supper, the wife asked, "What did you do about the mole?"

"Put out some poison," I said, chewing an asparagus spear.

"POISON!" she shrieked. "You put poison in our front lawn?"

"Certainly. You said you wanted me to get rid of the mole."

"But you didn't tell me you were going to poison the poor thing. That's downright inhumane…and besides, when the grandchildren visit us they may eat the poison. You know how inquisitive little Miles is. What kind of poison was it?"

"I think it was arsenic."

She made a choking noise. "I can't believe this. Why, it's…it's murder. Poor innocent little creature. Go right out and dig the poison up."

"Look," I said dramatically, "it's either poison or moles."

"Then let it be moles," she cried resolutely.

Later that night we went out in the front yard, and as she held a flashlight, I dug up the pellets. "I hope you're satisfied," I told her. "Albert Schweitzer would be proud of you."

Several days after that, I looked for traces of the mole, but couldn't find any. Apparently, it had decided that it was causing too much domestic discord—or maybe it ate some of the poison. Whatever the case, my Yankee wife hasn't forgiven me. "Poor little mole," she mumbles tenderly as we pass the remains of one of its mounds.

Which leaves me wondering: how did the Yankees manage to win the Civil War.

A Defense of Cockroaches

Cockroach season is approaching and, like many a Southern boy, I look forward to the return of these innocent and much maligned little creatures. My only problem is that cockroach season is the beginning of the inevitable battle between my wife and me. She detests cockroaches—but I find myself strangely attracted to them.

This battle goes back a long way. It began in the 1950's when I was living in New York and courting the girl who would eventually become my wife. In an attempt to "sell" her on the South, I told her stories about my native region, including accounts of the Southern cockroach. I realize now that this was bad psychology.

"Gosh, honey," I would say in as drippy a Southern accent as I could muster, "you just ought to see the cockroaches we have down there. There's nothing in New York to compare with them."

"Cockroaches?" she would reply, sniffing with disgust. "We don't have many of them up here, and I don't care for the ones I've seen."

"You'll get over that," I assured her. "I'll show you cockroaches like you've never seen before. You'll write home about them."

"How…how big are they?"

"I've seen one the size of a small dog," I replied, getting carried away by my subject. "Why, when I was a boy, dad and I used to put out Have-a-Heart traps to catch them. And they're smart. On one occasion I trained a cockroach to bring in the morning paper. If handled properly, cockroaches make good pets."

As I said earlier, it was bad psychology. I merely succeeded in frightening her. When we moved South, and she saw her first cockroach, she became hysterical. I found her up on a stool in the kitchen, screaming and brandishing a poker. "It's attacking me," she cried. "Do something."

The cockroach, in this case, was a feeble old creature with a pair of gray antennae that he waved at her in a vain attempt to make friends. He meant no harm. I spoke sharply to him, and he limped away disconsolately. "You've hurt his feelings," I said—but my wife went on screaming.

Next day I hired an exterminator—a likeable man who sympathized with my attitude toward cockroaches. "I can get rid of 'em for you," he said, "but to tell the truth I don't see no harm in them. Like any other critter, a cockroach will fight for its life if cornered—but I have yet to see one engage in an unprovoked attack."

"I agree," I told him. "Just pretend to spray around the house, but don't actually hurt them—or their progeny. I promise not to tell your boss."

The plan worked well for a few years, but at last the exterminator died and was replaced by a new exterminator—a cold, scientific killer who soon filled the house with carcasses of dead roaches. I felt as though I had hired a hit man. I fired him at once.

Now summer is coming, and my wife and I are preparing for our annual cockroach battle. She says my attitude toward cockroaches is that of a "bleeding heart liberal," while I accuse her of having the instincts of a serial killer. We argue constantly over the matter and can come to no agreement. We have considered divorce—but that would be too costly. I have written to Dr. Phil. I have talked the matter over with my pastor. There seems to be no answer.

Can this forty-five year old marriage between a Southern cockroach lover and a New York cockroach hater be saved?

Neurotic Raccoons and Other Problems

"Life," as Winston Churchill once said, "is just one damn thing after another." I agree. Last month I was complaining about my difficulties with cockroaches. This month it's raccoons. Always something!

About a year ago, a construction company cut down a forested area near our house, and a pair of raccoons (married, I presume) moved into our back yard. It wasn't long before the mother raccoon gave birth to three cunning little offspring, after which the whole family began coming up on our patio to eat the food we put out for our cat.

My wife and I didn't mind—at first. "Aren't they adorable!" the wife chortled. "They look like little bandits, with their funny masks and cute little ring tails."

"Yes," I agreed apprehensively, "they're charming. But they can be nuisances."

All went well for a while. Then word must have gotten around that my wife and I were a soft touch, because soon a second raccoon family took up residence in our back yard and signed on to the welfare role. Every evening about five o'clock, both families would hold a reunion on our patio—mothers, fathers, babies, grandparents, etc. They were dainty eaters—I'll give them that—but they left nothing for our cat, who began to lose weight and show signs of deep depression.

Our cat—I have written about him before—is a large and cowardly old tabby who has been hanging around our house for many years, stubbornly refusing to come indoors and act like a normal feline. He has no baptismal name: we call him "Big Boy." We have grown quite attached to the lovable old coward.

"We need another bag of cat food," the wife told me recently. "The raccoons have finished the old one off. The cat is starving."

"But I just bought a ten pound bag last week," I told her. "The cat has to learn to fight for his food—'survival of the fittest' and that sort of thing."

"Survival of the fittest!" she sneered. "What can one lone cat do against an army of raccoons? You need to think of something—and quickly."

Things went from bad to worse. As the raccoons gathered each evening for their meal, the cat would leap up on a ledge and bump against our kitchen window, meowing mournfully and giving us guilt-making looks. For a while, we tried feeding the raccoons first and feeding the cat later. But the raccoons saw through this little ploy quite easily and took to waiting around for seconds.

One night recently, as I watched the raccoons at their evening banquet, I had had enough. I grabbed a yard rake, ran out on the patio and began jabbing at them. They gazed at me with astonishment, and then backed away grudgingly, growling deep in their throats. It was a bit frightening.

When I came back indoors and explained things to my wife, I expected her to sympathize with me—but no!—she took the raccoons' part. "Of course they were disturbed," she said. "First you encourage them to come up on the patio and eat—and then you chase them away with a rake. You'll make them neurotic. One of these days they may even attack you. I don't know that I would blame them."

"But you told me to do something!" I said with annoyance.

"Yes," she said, "but I didn't tell you to upset the balance of nature." I made no reply. There's no way to deal with such irrationality.

So there you have the problem: a depressed cat, a band of neurotic raccoons and a wife who, like all members of the species, expects miracles of me. Once again, I appeal to my readers: you helped me with cockroaches—help me again with raccoons.

My Inflation Dream

Everybody has strange dreams once in a while, and most of us like to tell them to our wives, husbands, or close friends—which can be rather boring for our wives, husbands or close friends.

I bet that even Sigmund Freud had the occasional strange dream—and bored his wife telling it to her. I picture him dressed in his bathrobe, coming down to breakfast. "Goot morning, mine frau," he says. "Let me tell you de strange dream I had last night. I vas sitting on a park bench doing a crossvord puzzle ven suddenly dis little midget comes up to me and says…"

"Gott in Himmel," his wife thinks. "And he gets paid for listening to dis stuff."

Speaking of Freud, I disagree with his contention that all of our dreams are about sex. I dream about all sorts of things: the war in Iraq, athletes foot, the pants I forgot to pick up at the cleaners, inflation…especially inflation. Recently, for instance, I had a dream about inflation.

Like most strange dreams this one began peacefully enough. The alarm clock rang; I got out of bed, stumbled into the kitchen and sat down at the table. Suddenly, I noticed that my wife was floating around the ceiling with a coffee pot in her hand. As often happens in dreams, however, this didn't surprise me. "Morning, dear," I said placidly, glancing up at her. "Why are you floating around the ceiling?"

"Everything else is going up these days," she said. "Why shouldn't I?"

"Makes sense," I replied thoughtfully. "But come down long enough to fix my breakfast. I'll have scrambled eggs and bacon."

"Oh, you will, will you," she snarled, pouring a long stream of coffee into my cup. "I just came from the grocery, and I assure you it's a jungle out there. Eggs $146 a dozen. Bacon $200 a pound. From now on you're getting gruel for breakfast!"

"But what about my protein levels?" I cried. "I'll die without proper protein."

"I'll miss you!" she snapped unsympathetically. "Gasoline: $100 a gallon. Pecans: a dollar apiece—unshelled. Bathroom tissue: $50 a roll."

"Hmm," I said. "We *do* need bathroom tissue. Why not shop at Big Store where the prices are lower? If you're embarrassed to be seen there, wear a wig."

"Where do you think I've been shopping?" she asked. "Everybody goes to Big Store nowadays. Yesterday, I saw Laura Bush and Hillary Clinton in line ahead of me. You've got to come out of retirement. You've got to get a job!"

"Ridiculous," I muttered. "I'm old and sick. I have arthritis in both feet."

"But think of the children," she said, bursting into tears. "They're starving."

"That's their own fault," I replied. "They insisted on taking early retirement."

"You've got to get a job," she repeated. "Have you tried McDonalds?"

"Not McDonalds," I screamed. "I'm allergic to French Fried potatoes…"

I awoke to find my wife standing over my bed shaking me by the shoulder. "Wake up," she said. "You were having a nightmare. Your breakfast is ready—scrambled eggs and bacon."

"No! No!" I yelled. "Eggs are $146 a dozen. Bacon is $200 a pound. And come down from that ceiling. If you break a hip, they'll raise the premium on our insurance policy!"

Let Freud find any sex in that dream! Didn't they have inflation in Vienna?

My Favorite Diet

I was checking out at the supermarket recently when a headline on the cover of one of the Ladies Magazines caught my eye: "Reach Your Dream Weight—Lose 50 Pounds in Two Weeks." The article was by a woman named Felicia Fantail—which didn't sound too promising. Still, the title interested me. I've been a bit overweight lately, so why not give the diet a try? I bought the magazine.

When I got home and my wife saw the magazine she gave me an annoyed look. "Are you implying that I'm overweight?" she asked.

"Don't be paranoid," I replied calmly. "I bought the magazine for myself. I need to drop about 20 pounds. You're always telling me I'm too fat."

"Yes, you are," she admitted. "But when you go on a diet, it always puts you in a bad mood."

"So? Take your choice: a lean, mean mate, or a lovey, chubby hubby?"

"Couldn't we compromise on 'burly and slightly surly?'"

I read aloud from the article. "The key to weight loss is will power. Will power is everything. Without will power you will never achieve weight loss."

I gave my wife a triumphant look. "How about that?" I said. "You know what tremendous will power I have."

"I'm more familiar with your 'won't power,'" she replied, "especially when I ask you to cut the lawn."

Ignoring her, I settled down in an armchair to read the article. After a rather boring introduction, the author got down to what she called her "hip strip" diet.

"Breakfast: half a grapefruit, cup of black coffee, slice of unbuttered Melba toast. Lunch: half head of lettuce (no dressing), small carrot, one ounce roasted chicken, glass of distilled water. Dinner: slice of tomato, three ounces of lean hamburger, two Brussels sprouts. Between meal snack: all the parsley you want."

I shuddered with horror. "Someone should tell Dr. Kevorkian about this woman," I muttered. "She's invented a new method of assisted suicide."

Before throwing the magazine away in disgust, my eyes wandered to the next page where an ad for Campbell's Soup caught my attention. The ad contained a recipe for something called "Chicken Royale with Savory Dumplings." There was a picture of a mouth-watering casserole composed of chicken, bacon, and cheese, with clouds of steam bubbling through plump, succulent dumplings. "Hmm," I thought. "Interesting."

I thumbed through the magazine and came to an article entitled "Easy Sunday Night Specials." The first "special" was "Hungarian Goulash with Mushroom Gravy." Next came "Pork Chops stuffed with Roquefort Cheese." And finally, "Beef Wellington with Creamed Eggplant." I was beginning to salivate.

Finally, there was an article titled "Desserts to Please the Most Jaded Palates." I've never thought of myself as having a jaded palate, but the recipes looked intriguing: "Strawberry Supreme With Caramel Sauce," "Banana Cream Frappe" "Maraschino Cherry Delight" "Mousse Marzipan." I hummed to myself.

Just at that moment my wife walked through the room. "How's the diet coming?"

"Diet?" I muttered, like a man emerging from a trance. "What are you talking about? I've just discovered some of the greatest recipes that mankind ever achieved. I'm going out to buy more Ladies Magazines, and when I get back—clear the kitchen. Your lovey, chubby husband is about to begin a new form of dieting!"

New Car Fever: A Psychological Case Study

I am caught in the trammels of New Car Fever: a bounden slave to the horrors of this deadly disease. Although it usually strikes me in the summer, it came early this year, due to the clever machinations of the auto industry: rebates, zero financing, misleading advertisements and, of course, free popcorn and hot dogs.

I spend my time malingering about the premises of auto showrooms. I read the sticker prices. I talk to salesmen. I even prowl around the lot at midnight when the salesmen won't bother me. Instead of an array of gorgeous pin-up pictures that one might expect to find on the walls of my office, there are photos of the latest new car models. The thing has become an obsession.

My wife found me in the kitchen in this pitiable condition at 2 a.m. one morning. I had been up all night, pacing around the kitchen, drinking endless cups of coffee, popping B.C. Headache Powder and watching the roaches race across the floor. I was obviously on the verge of a nervous collapse.

"Still got New Car Fever," my wife asked, consternation showing on her face.

"Yes," I replied shakily. "I can't get the image of the new Wandango Hatchback out of my mind. I see it in my dreams: the sleek body lines, the over-sized racing tires, the plutonium air bags, the dual ashtrays with President Bush's picture on them. I must have a Wandango!"

"Well, why don't you just go down and buy one?"

"We can't afford it!" I screamed. "I can't even keep up the payments on that new toaster we bought at Bill's Dollar Store. Our budget is so fractured that it looks like a patient at an orthopedic clinic."

"That settles it!" she said decisively. "Tomorrow, I'm making you an appointment with your psychiatrist, Dr. Sigmund Hofflespinker. If anybody can help you, he can."

Ten o'clock next morning found me in Dr. Hofflespinker's waiting room, my teeth chattering, my hands trembling. There were three other patients in the office: a tall lanky man who was standing on his head in the corner reciting "The Raven;" an elderly lady walking around the office on a pair of stilts; and a muscular young man who wore a loin cloth and occasionally gave the Tarzan yell. I paid no attention to them. I had problems of my own.

When the time came for my appointment, a nurse led me into Dr. Hofflespinker's office. He was a short, fat man with a purple goatee and pince-nez glasses. He was smoking two cigars at once and working a crossword puzzle.

"Ah, goot morning," he said soothingly, studying my chart and checking my insurance. "Pliss lie down on de couch und tell old Dr. Hofflespinker de problem." He smiled kindly, double-checking my insurance.

"Doc," I said, clutching my throat, "I've got New Car Fever. All day long I think of nothing except that new car made by the Chow Mein Motor Works. You've heard of it, perhaps: the Wandango—a seven door hatchback with a 15.6 liter engine, 10 speed transmission, anti-lock bumper guards, dual controls and plutonium wheel covers. Unfortunately, it costs $75,000. I can't afford such a price—but I can't get the car off my mind. I'm going mad…mad, I tell you."

"Dis iss a common complaint," he said, blowing a pair of double smoke rings.

"Effrybody gets New Car Fever at one time or anudder. Mother Theresa, Billy Graham und even the great Sigmund Freud suffered from it. I had an attack myself once." He studied me carefully through half closed eyes. "You say the car costs $75,000. Dot sounds like a bargain. Does it haf a zebra striped steering wheel?"

"Yes, yes!" I cried, drooling.

"Vot about a tachometer?"

"A gold plated tachometer with a halogen bulb."

"Do you mind telling me de name of de dealer?"

I told him. He got up from his chair, jammed his hat on his head and rushed toward the door. "Doc," I screamed after him, "come back. You've got to help me…"

"All in goot time," he yelled back. "But first I must purchase one of dose Vandangos. Come back tomorrow for annuder visit. Und I must warn you dat I am doubling my fee. Somehow I got to pay for de car. Auf Wiedersehen!"

Confessions of a
Professional Car Loser

Whenever I go to the Mall, I invariably forget where I parked my car. This is not only frustrating, but also embarrassing, since people notice me roaming around the parking lot and offer to help. Apparently there is something in the situation that brings out the "helpful" side of human nature. I suppose it's the same instinct that makes people remind you that you have left your car lights on or gleefully point out the fact that you are going the wrong way on a one way street. I don't know whether this represents a good or a bad side of human nature. The question is too deep for me.

A typical example of this odd phenomenon happened to me recently on a broiling day in August. I had gone to the Mall to do some shopping, and when I came outside to look for my car I realized that—sure enough—I had forgotten where I parked it. As I began searching the parking lot, a fat lady wearing a blonde wig approached me. "Can't find your car?" she asked.

"No," I admitted with a false smile. "I must be getting Alzheimer's Disease!"

"I've did it a hundred times myself," she said. "I'll help you look fer it."

"Oh, that's too much trouble..."

"No trouble a-tall. What kind of a car was it?"

At that moment, I felt someone tugging at my sleeve. Looking down, I saw a young kid in a Boy Scout uniform. "Lost your car, mister?" he asked brightly.

"Yes," I muttered. "But I'm sure I can find it..."

"I'll help you," he said, with a big grin. "My good deed for the day."

An elderly gentleman wearing a hearing aid and carrying a cane shuffled up beside me. "Lose your car?" he asked in a loud voice.

"Yes. But I think I can…"

"Betcha somebody stole it," he said. "Ain't nothing safe these days. I'll hep you look fer it. Two heads is better than one! Heh, heh!"

I heard a horn beeping behind me. It was the Mall Security Van. "Misplaced your car, young feller?" the uniformed driver asked with an amused smile.

"Er…yes," I muttered, slightly annoyed at the irony of being called "young feller."

"Hop in," he said, patting the seat beside him. "We'll find it."

"Somebody probably stole it," the elderly gentleman shouted as we pulled away. "I seen a feller running down the street carrying a pair of pliers. Betcha he stole it!"

We drove around the lot for about ten minutes. The elderly man and the Boy Scout waved cheerfully to us. As we passed the fat lady, she flagged us down. "I done searched every row," she said. "Are you sure you parked in *this* lot?"

At her words, an icy pang of embarrassment ran down my spine. "I…I remember now," I mumbled. "I left it in the parking lot on the other side of the Mall."

Without a word, the security guard revved up his motor and drove in silence to the other lot. I tried to chat with him on the way, but he wasn't having any of it. After we found the car, I thanked him, but he only nodded sullenly. "Next time, you need to remember where you parked," he said. "Feller can waste a lot of time this way!"

"I'm sorry about that," I replied as he drove off.

I don't think I'll go to the Mall alone anymore. It's too embarrassing. In fact, I don't think I'll go anywhere alone anymore. I'll just stay home and watch television.

If only I can remember where I put that remote control!

Strategies for Saving on Gas

I came in the house screaming for my wife—like Marlon Brando in *A Streetcar Named Desire.*

"What's wrong dear?" she asked, giving me a suspicious glance.

"What makes you think anything's wrong?" I replied.

"Well, for one thing your face is bright red. For another, your eyes are crossed. And finally, your Adams Apple is doing the hula, hula!"

"Quite the little Sherlock Holmes, aren't you," I said sarcastically. "But you're right. I'm worried about the rising price of gas. I just filled up the old jalopy—and practically had to take out a second mortgage on the house to pay the tab."

"Yes," she said. "Everybody in the neighborhood is worried. The Jones swapped their Cadillac for a bicycle-built-for-two, the Smiths just went by on pogo sticks, and old Mr. Plumby is in his back yard shooting for oil—like Jed Clampert."

"Stop trying to be funny, sweetheart," I said. "We need to have a serious talk about ways to save on gas."

"I hate it when you call me 'Sweetheart,'" she said. "It always means you're about to blame me for something."

"Well, you're the chief culprit. Today, for instance, you made five trips to Big Store, four trips to Banjo's Supermarket, and two trips to Cheapo Dress Shoppe!"

"True enough," she admitted. "But it was only because I kept remembering things I had forgotten to buy. Besides, you're as much to blame as me. I counted five trips you made to Home Depot this morning."

"That was because I kept getting the wrong size washer. It could happen to anybody. But let's stop blaming each other and figure out some ways to save gas."

"Well," she said after a moment's thought, "we could buy a large square rigger sail, attach it to the hood of the car, and…"

"Might work," I agreed. "Better still, we could coast to Big Store by way of Maple Street and then coast back by way of Oak Street."

"That's impossible," she said. "It would mean breaking the law of gravity."

"So—we break a few laws. Just make sure the cops aren't watching!"

She drummed her fingers on the table. "I have it!" she exclaimed. "How about we buy a glider, haul it up on the roof and glide to the store?"

"Wouldn't work," I said. "The roof already has too many leaks. But you've given me an idea. You know how we've always laughed at those crazy schemes of Wiley E. Coyote on 'Road Runner.' Well, maybe some of them are not so crazy.

For instance, we could put on roller skates, strap torpedoes to our sides and propel ourselves down the street. Or maybe get a massive sling shot and…"

"Be serious," she said. "At your age, they'd arrest you for Alzheimer's Disease."

We thought it over for a while. "I've got the answer," I said at last. "But you're not going to like it."

"Give it to me straight."

"We go out on the sidewalk, put the right foot forward, then the left foot…"

"You mean…?"

"Exactly. It's an ancient form of transportation. It's called—walking!"

Some Explosive Evening

I rarely go to the movies anymore. In the first place they cost too much. In the second place, I can't understand them. The old classics, like "Casablanca," "It's a Wonderful Life," or "Lassie Come Home," were easy to follow. They had plot, plausible dialogue and actors I was familiar with. Today's movies have none of the above. I've never heard of any of the stars (they change about once a month), the dialogue strikes me as idiotic, and the plots consist mainly of "special effects." In fact, unless I have some young person with me to explain what is happening, I become hopelessly lost.

Here is my impression of a movie I watched recently with my son. I think it was called "The Mummy Has Quadruplets."

Opening Scene: We are flying over the Himalayan Mountains. It is not clear what sort of vehicle we are flying in—but it doesn't seem to matter. Without the slightest introduction, the movie has started. The music is deafening. Suddenly, the names of the "stars" float up on the screen: Nicole Kidman, Angelina Jolie, George Clooney, Russell Crowe, and Leonardo DiCaprio! Who are these people and what do they want? I'm already confused. How about some real "stars"—like Clark Gable, Bette Davis, Jimmy Stewart or Shirley Temple? It would help put us old-timers at ease!

As we continue flying over the Himalayas, we witness the first "special effect." One of the mountains—probably Mount Everest—explodes. Dust, rocks and trees fly around the screen.

"Wow!" says my son. "How about that for a special effect!"

I'm more puzzled than impressed, but I try not to let him know it. "Yes, that's...amazing. I wonder how they did it? Built a small scale model of Mount Everest, I suppose."

"No," he says, "actually they built a 29,000 foot replica of Mount Everest—like they did for the ocean liner in *Titanic*. The film won an Oscar for special effects."

Scene 2: Two cars are engaged in what I believe is called a "high-speed chase." They leap drawbridges, zoom along crowded highways and sideswipe telephone poles. Meanwhile, the passengers inside the cars fire rockets at each other. The first car explodes. The second car explodes. The other cars on the highway explode. The highway explodes. Since there seems to be nothing left to explode, the scene ends. Thanks heavens! All these explosions rattle me.

"That was Angelina Jolie and George Clooney in the first car and Nicole Kidman and Russell Crowe in the second," my son explains. "Aren't they great?"

"Er…yes…but what did all that have to do with the opening scene set in the Himalayas?"

"Simple. Kidman and Crowe are spies. They plan to blow up the world. Jolie and Clooney are CIA agents trying to stop them."

"But how did you know that?"

"You have to sort of figure things out for yourself!"

Scene 3: New York City. Crowds of people strolling along the streets. A truck hurtles by, the driver leaps out and the truck explodes. The people on the street begin to explode. The camera pans to the Empire State Building—which also explodes. Kidman and Crowe are shown kissing passionately. Suddenly Crowe explodes.

"That was Leonardo DiCaprio driving the truck," my son explains.

"Why didn't he explode?"

"Don't be silly, Dad. He's an android. An android can't explode."

"But Crowe exploded."

"He wasn't an android. Just watch the movie. You'll figure things out."

More special effects follow, mostly explosions. The Golden Gate Bridge explodes. A Wal-Mart store explodes. The Pentagon explodes. The entire continent of Africa explodes. The movie ends with Kidman and DiCaprio kissing passionately.

"I thought Kidman was in love with Crowe," I venture.

"Crowe exploded, remember? How did you like the special effects?"

"Er…great. But I would have liked a little more plot."

"Who cares about plot when you have such awesome special effects?"

I suppose this sort of thing appeals to you if you've been raised on it. My son tells me the picture grossed $100 million. But I'll stick to "Casablanca," "It's a Wonderful Life," and "Lassie, Come Home."

Much less explosive.

A Guide to Fixing Toilets
For Dummies

Before we were married, I explained quite clearly to my wife that I was no good at home repairs. "I know nothing about machinery," I told her. "Tools hold no interest for me. Auto mechanics laugh at me, TV repairmen giggle at me, and clerks at the Do It Yourself Store actually try to talk me out of projects. Let there be no deception: if you marry me you will be marrying the Village Idiot of the Industrial Age."

After thinking it over, she agreed to take me anyway. "My father was never good at fixing things," she said, "but he learned. Perhaps you will too."

Well, the years have passed, and I haven't learned. My only consolation is that I am a little better at fixing things than my wife is. On a scale of one to ten, her mechanical ability can only be described by the use of negative numbers. Consequently, I am occasionally able to impress her with the few bits of knowledge that I have learned through the years. For instance, I'm pretty good with toilets.

My wife came to me recently with a toilet problem. It was ten o'clock at night—generally the hour when things decide to get broken at my house.

"I wish you'd look at the toilet in the middle bathroom," she said as I lay comfortably in bed reading a book.

"I've seen it many times," I replied, looking up from my book.

"Something's definitely wrong," she said, ignoring my sarcasm. "It hasn't worked for two days."

"What seems to be the trouble?" I asked, ruefully laying the book down.

"I'm not sure. I think the motor is broken. I tried to fix it with the force plunger, but I couldn't."

This propelled me into an upright position. "Look," I explained patiently, "a toilet doesn't have a motor. A toilet works by the principle of gravity."

"I'm sure I don't know anything about that," she replied. "I only know something is wrong with it. The water doesn't get pushed down hard enough. The flush is weak."

"The water doesn't get *pushed* down at all," I explained, "nor can you say the 'flush is weak.' The water falls by its own weight. All water weighs the same. What undoubtedly is wrong is that the drain is stopped up. You say it hasn't worked for two days? It was exactly two days ago that our daughter and the grandchildren left."

"Well, you needn't try to blame it on them. Several months ago, I found Little Miles dropping pecans down the toilet and I cautioned him against it. I can assure you he hasn't been near it since then."

Without more ado, I went into the laundry room, found the force plunger and returned to the bathroom. I flushed the toilet a couple of times to satisfy myself that the drain was, indeed, stopped up. Then I immersed the plunger in the water at the bottom of the bowl and let it fill up. I knew this was where my wife had made her mistake. She pushes the plunger in the toilet and flails away madly. Actually, you must first let the plunger fill up with water. That's the secret of it.

I pumped away for about a minute, and then, after gurgling and moaning painfully, the toilet began reluctantly to surrender its contents. First, a small rubber comb bubbled up, followed by a typewriter eraser, a blue crayon, a soggy book of matches and finally a "Happy Face" button. A good catch, I thought. I flushed the toilet twice to make sure it worked properly and then sauntered casually into the bedroom.

"It's working," I told my wife.

"What was wrong with it?" she asked.

"It's too technical to explain," I told her.

"Sometimes you can be pretty clever," she said. "You've learned a lot through the years."

I climbed into bed and picked up my book. We husbands must capitalize on small victories.

The Satanic TV Set

The main trouble with the modern world is that all the gadgets intended to make life easier—cell phones, VCRs, digital watches, computers, etc.—actually end up making life more complicated. For example, take the new TV set I just bought.

My old set (a console model) was thirty years old and dated from the days of Lawrence Welk, Richard Nixon, Bing Crosby and Nat King Cole. (Younger readers may want to look these names up in the encyclopedia.) It was a massive and beautiful piece of furniture: six feet long and five feet tall. It had a 12-inch picture tube. I loved it.

But through the years it had developed problems. The colors were rather odd. Lou Dobbs' face was green, Oprah Winfrey's hair was purple, and Wolf Blitzer's beard was orange. And there were some distortions in the picture tube. David Letterman's head was larger than his body, and Jay Leno's chin stretched down to the bottom of the screen. Reluctantly, I decided to donate the old set to Goodwill and buy a new one.

The new set was an ugly thing: a square slab of gray metal with a dull twenty-seven inch screen and a puzzling little instrument called a "remote control"—which reminded me of a pocket calculator undergoing an identity crisis.

After the set was delivered, I thumbed through the Instruction Manual. It was written in English, French, and Polish and, I think, Swahili. I turned to the section titled "Auto Set Up Menu." That sounded simple enough—but wasn't. It consisted of a series of bewildering terms: Micron Icon (nice rhyme), Variable Navigation (added, no doubt, for Sea Captains), and something called SAP (obviously the manufacturer's attempt at humor.)

I decided to jump right into things. I plugged the set in, pushed the Power Button and waited expectantly for the picture. The set groaned as if in pain, and the screen filled with snowflakes. I pressed the Menu button. The set made a burping noise and a yellow box appeared: "Recall Mode, Clock Set, Sleep Timer, Color Tint, and Idioma Langue." These sounded interesting but not exactly what I was looking for.

My wife came into the room. "Having trouble?" she asked.

"Nothing I can't handle," I assured her, pressing more buttons. A pink dinosaur appeared, dancing with some odd looking children.

"Oh, there's Barney," my wife chortled. "The grandchildren love him."

"Really?" I said sarcastically. "I don't share their feelings. He makes me understand why dinosaurs are extinct."

I pressed the "Search Mode" button, and the set began to change channels on its own. I watched a young man with an Australian accent holding the jaws of a crocodile apart, two hunters firing at a formation of geese, King Kong gazing at Fay Wray, and Mother Angelica scowling at me!

I pressed the "Idioma Langue" button and got the Beverly Hillbillies speaking in Spanish. I hit the channel changer and got Garth Brooks singing in French! When I squeezed the Volume Control, an unearthly howl split my ears.

I banged my head against the wall. I wanted my old set back. I wanted Jay Leno's elongated chin, David Letterman's oversized head, and Wolf Blitzer's orange beard. I felt as frustrated as an infant attempting to get its big toe out of its mouth.

But all is not lost. I have hit on a desperate plan of action. Tomorrow, I intend to return to Goodwill, buy back my old set, and give them the new one. So what if they give me odd looks? At least I'll retain my sanity!

Gadget Me No More
Gadgets, Please!

This Christmas my oldest son and his family came to visit us from Austin, Texas, where my son works for a computer firm. I haven't the faintest idea what he does, although he has explained it to me a dozen times. All I know is that it has something to do with "firewalls" and "viruses"—which sounds like a cross between Smokey the Bear and an HMO primary physician. (It's embarrassing for me to be unable to tell people what my son does for a living. I always get the feeling that they'll think I'm covering up for him—that maybe he's a bank robber or a bookie.)

When he visits us, he brings us all sorts of technological devices: a Walkman, a digital camera, a VCR and other weird fruits of modern technology.

This year he brought us a wireless telephone—the kind you carry around the house with you. The thing looked like the combination of a miniature flying saucer, a pocket calculator and the handle of an ornate flyswatter. It had a keyboard with rows of numbers on it, a screen that lit up when you removed the phone from its holder, and an assortment of oddly named buttons that I still don't understand—things like "rev" "memo" "skip" "flash" and "delete."

Beaming with pride, my son placed the phone in a prominent spot on my desk. I really didn't want it there, but I didn't want to hurt his feelings. I didn't like the looks of the thing. I would have preferred to put it in a less obvious place.

"Maybe we should put it somewhere other than my desk," I said tactfully. "When the grandkids come they might break it."

"Nah," he said. "It's rugged. They can't hurt it." So there was nothing to do except leave it on my desk—at least during his visit.

He then began to explain to me how to use the thing. "First trick," he said, "is to learn how to answer it. Pick it up and press the 'talk' button. O.K?"

I picked it up, pressed the 'talk' button and waited. "It's not talking," I said.

"Of course not, Dad. Nobody has called you. How about I call you on my cell phone?"

He whipped out his cell phone and pushed a couple of buttons. My new phone began to ring. "Go ahead. Answer it," my son said.

I picked the thing up and held it gingerly in my hand—the way you might hold a newborn baby. "What hath God wrought?" I asked while it continued to ring.

My wife, who was at the other end of the house, screamed: "Somebody answer the phone."

"You have to push the 'talk' button," my son said. I began a feverish search of buttons, and out of sheer desperation, pressed one—the wrong one, it appears. An electronic voice said "You have no new messages," and the phone began to ring again.

"Somebody get that phone," my wife screamed again. "It may be the pest control man. He's due today."

At that instant, an operator's voice came on again: "If you wish to make a call, please hang up and try again."

I handed the phone to my son. "Here," I cried. "Take the thing—take it back to Austin. I don't think Alexander Graham Bell himself could work it. Your mother and I will stick to that old black rotary phone in the kitchen. There's a limit to how much technology a man can absorb without going insane!"

Taxing Tactics

Back in the 1980's, the IRS audited my tax returns five years in succession. I was never quite sure why. I admit I don't look too honest—but then neither did Abraham Lincoln. The whole thing was stressful. I finally reached the point where I scheduled a session with a psychiatrist after each audit. (I was able to take it as a deduction the following year.)

If you have ever been audited, you know that the procedure is not exactly "fun and games." The stool they made me sit on, the intense light they shone in my face, and the rubber hose on the auditor's desk were distracting. Nor did it help when the auditor handed me a can of deodorant and said, "You may need this before the interview is over."

He was a large man, conservatively dressed in somber black. I could tell that he wanted to keep a psychological distance between us. For instance, he addressed me by my social security number.

"Do you swear to tell the truth, the whole truth and nothing but the truth?" he asked.

"Y...yes, all of the above," I stuttered. "I've never lied to anybody—except my wife, of course."

"Excellent. Now, I'm going inject you with a shot of sodium pentothal—better known as truth serum."

I rolled up my sleeve, and he stuck me with the needle. I fainted briefly, and he revived me with a few slaps.

"Hmm," he muttered, studying my tax return with a magnifying glass, "On Line 1 of the return, you state that your income last year was $500. That seems a bit small? How do you explain it?"

"Well, you see, I was fired from my job."

"What was your job?"

"I worked for a mattress company. They accused me of lying down on the job." It was an attempt at lightening the tense atmosphere with a dash of humor.

"We don't encourage humor," he snarled. "All right. Let's go on. I see that on Line 15 you list your wife as a dependent. Does she have any visible means of support?"

"Only a girdle." I said with a painful smile.

"I told you we don't encourage humor," he said, breaking one of my fingers. "O.K. Please look at Line 21. It says: 'Take your gross income and divide by 9. Subtract this amount from Line 8. Multiply by Line 30. Add 200. This will give you the exact day, month and year in which you were born.' What do you think of that?"

"Amazing," I said, with a sneer in my voice.

"Do I detect sarcasm?" he asked, breaking another finger. "That brings us to Line 52. It says: 'Put your hand in your pocket and count the change. If the amount is less than your yearly income, you owe the government the difference.' According to my calculations you owe $1200. Please pay the cashier on the way out. See you next year!"

Next day I hired a CPA to do my taxes. He tells me that he too now schedules a psychiatric appointment after each audit. Poor guy, I know how he feels!

A Postal Social

One of the nice things about being retired is that you find time for the work you couldn't do when you were working! Now that I'm retired, I find a million errands to do, most of them the products of my wife's teeming brain.

Recently, for instance, she sent me to the post office to buy a book of stamps. This seemed like a simple task—one that even I could handle. The only thing that troubled me was that I knew I would have to face an enormous line. The last time I went to the post office I had an hour's wait. The memory of that ordeal troubled me. But I steeled myself this time and decided to face the problem bravely.

I drove to the post office, parked my car, and went in. I expected to find a long line—but I didn't expect to find an army. The line extended out of the doors, into the lobby, and spilled over into the parking lot.

"A bit busy," I said to an elderly lady ahead of me.

"You should have seen it an hour ago. They actually had a cop directing traffic."

"Where is the cop now when we need him?"

"He got trampled by the crowd and had to be taken away by ambulance."

An hour later, we had passed through the lobby and were inside the postal office itself. The crowd wound round and round, like an enormous boa constrictor. Behind the main desk stood one lone clerk—who was working like a beaver on amphetamines.

"Wonder what's causing all the delay?" I asked a man in front of me who was working a crossword puzzle.

"It's all these labor saving devices," he replied, studying the puzzle. "Say, maybe you can help me. Can you think of a six letter word that means 'cowardly?'"

I thought for a minute. "How about 'craven,'" I suggested.

"That'll work. Thanks a lot."

A lady two places ahead of me was writing a letter. "I'll be finished by the time I get to the clerk," she said with a pleasant smile. "I always wait to start my letters until I get to the post office. Saves time."

Four ladies in the line ahead had set up a card table and were playing bridge. As the line inched forward, I could hear them talking: "I bid three clubs, etc." They seemed to be enjoying themselves.

Meanwhile, the clerk had disappeared into the back office, but nobody seemed to notice. Everybody was too busy socializing.

"I need an eight letter word that means 'an ant eating animal found in Africa," the crossword puzzle man said.

"How about 'aardvark?'" I suggested.

"That fits," he said gratefully.

The letter-writing lady went on mumbling to herself. "Jimmy was up on the stepladder painting the house and spilled a bucket of paint on Grandpa. Wish you could see Stella. She has a new set of false teeth. They look awful!"

A man behind me began to sing "Sweet Adeline," in a deep bass voice. A few seconds later he was joined by a fat man who sang the tenor part. In less than a minute two other men had joined in. They sang in close harmony, like a barbershop quartet.

The bridge playing ladies were still at it. "I bid five spades," one of them said.

By this time, the clerk had returned but nobody noticed. Everybody was having too good a time. It was like a party or a family reunion. A group of young people began a game of charades. A young girl held up three fingers to indicate a three-syllable word and began to act out the syllables. We all watched with interest. "I've got it!" a fat lady cried. "The word is 'bigamy.'" We all applauded.

The quartet sang: "You are the flower of your time…Sweet Adeline."

"I pass," said one of the bridge ladies.

By this time I had reached the clerk's desk. I tried to remember why I had come, but couldn't. I panicked. "I'll be back in minute," I said, bolting for the door.

As I left, everybody told me goodbye. The quartet broke into "Auld Lang Syne." The crossword puzzle man tipped his hat. The writing lady flourished her pen. The bridge players and the charade group waved to me. I felt I was leaving old friends.

Yes, going to the post office these days can be a social occasion. You might as well learn to enjoy it.

A Simple Operation

Recently, I visited my friend Homer Doppleman, who had just undergone a minor hernia operation. The last time I talked to him, he assured me that the operation was "no big deal," so I was surprised to see him lying in bed and groaning with pain.

"Gosh, Homer," I said. "The operation must have been worse than expected."

"It wasn't the operation," he replied with an agonized shudder. "It was something worse—something too horrible to talk about."

"Maybe talking will help," I suggested. "Why don't you tell me about it."

"Well, all right," he said, bracing himself. "The story begins about a year ago when I went to see my doctor for my regular check-up. My HMO—it's called *Memento Mori*—allows me one check-up every ten years. I paid the clerk the $20 co-pay and spent five hours in the waiting room reading old copies of the *Wholesale Druggist's Digest*. After that, I was weighed, finger printed, strip searched and shuffled through a series of cubicles filled with more copies of the *Wholesale Druggist's Digest*.

"The doctor was out of breath when he came in—he'd been running from cubicle to cubicle. He examined me briefly, found a small hernia, asked for a $20 co-pay and scheduled an appointment for me with a surgeon named Dr. Ventrix Slicer.

"I had to wait three months to see Dr. Slicer. When the three months had elapsed, I went to his office, gave his clerk a $20 co-pay, waited five hours, was weighed, finger printed, strip searched and shuffled through another series of cubicles filled with old copies of the *Wholesale Druggist's Digest*. At last Dr. Slicer arrived—out of breath. He said I needed an MRI before he could operate. I had to wait two months for an appointment at the MRI clinic.

"When the time of my appointment finally arrived, the clerk demanded a $20 co-pay, gave me a copy of the *Wholesale Druggist's Digest* to read, and told me that before I could get the MRI I would need referrals from my primary care physician, my surgeon, two nurses and a janitor. Getting the referrals took another two months. When it was time for the MRI, I paid $20 co-pay, read the *Wholesale Druggist's Digest* for five hours, was strip-searched and squeezed into the MRI—a device that resembled the Black Hole of Calcutta. I paid another $20 co-pay, staggered home and collapsed.

"Two months later, it was time for the hernia operation by Dr. Slicer. I paid a $20 co-pay, read the *Wholesale Druggist's Digest* for five hours, was shuffled through the usual series of cubicles and finally saw Dr. Slicer. "You're Mr. Phillip Waxheimer, aren't you," he said, "and you're here to have an ear removed?"

"No, I'm Homer Doppleman—I'm here for a hernia operation."

"These glitches occur," he muttered, humming Beethoven's *Ninth Symphony*. The operation took ten minutes. "You're o.k." he said when it was over. "Drink lots of fluids, eat nothing for six days, and don't forget your $20 co-pay."

"Two days later, I got a letter from my HMO. 'This is not a bill,' it said, 'although it may look like a bill. The charge for your MRI is $5000. Your insurance will not pay this amount, since the proper referrals were not backdated. You also owe $6000 for your hernia operation, which is not covered under your policy. Your total bill is $25,000. Medi-Care will pay 10% of this amount, but you owe the remaining 90%. If you have already paid, ignore this letter.'"

"So what did you do?" I asked.

"I had a nervous breakdown, lost my job, and my wife divorced me. Life seemed scarcely worth living—so I called Dr. Kevorkian about getting an assisted suicide."

"And what did Dr. Kevorkian say?"

"He said that when I came to his office I would need a referral from my HMO, a $20 co-pay, and a few copies of the *Wholesale Druggist's Digest*."

Advanced Math for Seniors

A few days ago, I dropped by the house of my friend Homer Doppleman. The poor guy is in terrible shape—a regular walking dictionary of medical terms. He has a deviated septum, bronchitis, diverticulosis, hives, and emphysema, yeast allergy, arthritis, acid reflux, Plantar's Wart, and several other ailments that the doctors haven't been able to diagnose. He takes so many prescription drugs that his bathroom looks like a chemical laboratory.

"How you doing, Homer, old pal?" I asked jovially, slapping him on the back.

"Not so good," he replied, coughing loudly and beckoning me to a seat. His desk was piled high with pocket calculators, slide rules, graph paper, math textbooks, aspirin tablets, ice packs—and a bottle of Jack Daniels.

"Doing your income taxes early?" I asked.

"Nope," he replied, sweating profusely. "Trying to figure out the new Medicare Bill Congress just passed."

"What's the problem? Is the bill complicated?"

"Complicated isn't the word! It's so complicated that the White House had to bring in three Harvard professors to try to explain it to President Bush—and two them had nervous breakdowns. In fact, the bill has created such a crisis that the Director of Homeland Security plans to issue an orange alert."

"How does the bill work?"

"That's the trouble—nobody is sure. If you sign up for coverage, you have to shell out a monthly fee of $35. Twelve times $35 is $420. Then you have to pay a $250 deductible. The $250 deductible plus $420 comes to $670. You with me so far?"

"I think so," I said, adding up the amounts on my fingers.

"After that, Medicare pays 75% of the first $2,250. So $2250 minus $670 leaves $1580. If you take 75% of $1580 you get $1185."

"So Medicare pays $1185," I said.

"Not necessarily. Your HMO may already be paying more than $1185."

"How can you tell?" I asked.

"You can't. It's hidden somewhere in the small print. You need an electronic microscope to figure it out."

"So how much is the average Senior Citizen going to have to pay?"

"Like I said: nobody knows. I saw a projection from a government bureau claiming the bill would benefit any household containing 1.7 Senior Citizens."

"How can a household contain 1.7 Senior Citizens?"

"Maybe they cut off the leg of one of the citizens," he suggested.

"How do the drug companies feel about the bill?"

"They're not sure about it, but they're planning a big celebration anyway: champagne, caviar, and dancing girls dressed like aspirin tablets."

"What about doctors?"

"They haven't figured the thing out either. Too busy with malpractice suits."

"So who will the bill actually benefit?" I asked.

"Immigrants from the Near East. They're good at math. The government plans to hire thousands of them to teach courses in Higher Math for Senior Citizens."

"But I failed Math 101," I said.

"Me too. Care to borrow my bottle of Jack Daniels?"

Computer Language

I know very little about computers—but my wife knows even less. To her, computers are mysterious objects fraught with danger. She's terrified of them. The fact that I know just slightly more than she does about them gives me a pleasant feeling of superiority. I hope she never learns the truth.

Recently, we had a bad lightning storm in the neighborhood. Next morning at breakfast my wife said, "Your computer is making a funny noise. I'm afraid it's going to set the house on fire."

"I'll have a look at it," I said sagely. "Probably just some simple problem."

I went in my study and turned the thing on. "You have committed an illegal action," the monitor informed me. "Press the Tool Bar and, while holding it down, activate Book Ends. Then go directly to jail. Do not pass Go. Do not collect $200. Be careful not to erase the hard drive. If you have questions, call 911."

"Something wrong here," I decided with my usual alacrity. I called a local computer firm. "I'm having trouble with my computer," I told the clerk. "Either *it's* having a nervous breakdown—or I am. Better send somebody out to look at it."

A few hours later a pleasant young service man arrived. He unscrewed the back of the computer and removed a plastic gizmo full of wires and knobs. "It's your modem," he said, handing it to me. "The lightening storm must have burnt it out."

"Looks like it," I muttered, having no earthly idea what a modem was. "I never saw a modem so totally burnt out. It's a wonder it didn't set the house on fire."

He gave me a puzzled glance. "While I'm at it, do you want me to have a look at your Mother Board?"

"Good idea," I said. "And you might have a look at the Father Board too."

He gave me another puzzled look and tried to laugh. "That's pretty good," he said with a strained smile. "Mother Board…Father Board. Pretty funny." He tinkered with the thing a while. "I think there's Spywear in your computer," he said at last.

"Spyware?" I said. "Sounds serious. Shouldn't we report it to the FBI?"

He glanced at me to see if I was joking. When he realized I was serious, he said: "Spyware doesn't have anything to do with spies. It's sort of like a virus. I can put in a Firewall to protect your computer against it."

"Great," I said. "The more protection I have against fires, the better."

He mumbled something under his breath and tinkered with the set some more.

"I notice that you don't have a CD Burner," he said. "Want me to install one?"

"I don't think so," I replied. "I might forget to turn the CD Burner off, and it might burn the house down."

He gave me a blank look.

"By the way," I said, "did you check the hard drive? It's felt kind of soft lately."

"It's…it's o.k." he said hastily and handed me the bill.

As I wrote out the check, he said: "My company gives private tutorials for people who want to learn about computers. Would you be interested?"

"No," I told him. "I already have a pretty good understanding of the basics."

When he was gone, my wife asked: "What was wrong with your computer?"

"Too complex to explain," I told her. "The guy had to put in a Firewall."

"Good," she said. "I knew that computer was about to set the house on fire."

"Right," I agreed. "I caught it just in time!"

All God's Chillun Got Shoes

This is a column about shoes—not the conventional kind people of my generation wore, but those weird new sport shoes kids wear these days. I don't know quite how to describe them. I'm not even sure they should be called shoes. They look more like loaves of sourdough bread, or perhaps armadillos.

Recently, my teen-age granddaughter was having a birthday, so my wife sent me out to buy her a present.

"You might want to get her a pair of those new sport shoes all the kids are wearing," she said. "Be sure to get them wide enough. She has a very broad foot. I think a 7E should do it."

I went to a local shoe store where I was greeted in lackluster fashion by a young clerk who was talking on a mobile phone. He had a red goatee, a metal ring in his nose, and wore a T-shirt that said: "Do Random Acts of Kindness to Endangered Species." He seemed annoyed that I had disturbed his conversation.

"What's up, Pops?" he asked, reluctantly laying the phone down.

"I want to buy a pair of sport shoes for my granddaughter," I replied.

"What kind of sport shoes, Pops? We got running shoes, basketball shoes, volleyball shoes, hiking shoes, track shoes…"

"I'm not sure. My wife mentioned a brand called Nighties…or something."

"You mean Nikes. Sounds like you want running shoes. What size?"

"She has a very wide foot. Maybe a 7E."

"They don't come in different widths, Pops. Just different lengths. You'll have to buy a real long shoe to get the right width. Maybe a 12 or 13."

He removed a box from the shelf and lifted out two shapeless pieces of white rubber that looked big enough to fit a Tyrannosaurus Rex.

"They look a bit long," I said dubiously. "I'm afraid the toes would curl up—like something an elf might wear."

"So? She can wear three or four pairs of sox to take up the extra toe length."

"How much are they?"

"Hundred and fifty bucks," he said as nonchalantly as Donald Trump naming his price for the Taj Mahal.

I felt a shock run through my body. "Look," I explained, "when I was a kid my folks used to take me to Penney's every fall and buy me a pair of what, in those days, we referred to as tennis shoes. They cost a dollar and fifty cents a pair."

"Times have changed, Pops. This ain't the Middle Ages. Look at all the features these babies have. See this air pocket under the heel? It's filled with helium gas. The manufacturers originally used hydrogen, but the shoes kept exploding, so they substituted helium. And look at that sole. It contains hundreds of tiny springs that allow you to bounce up and down like a trampoline. And the left shoe contains a small AM/FM radio. She can listen to rock music as she runs. These shoes are awesome, Pops."

A hundred and fifty dollars for a pair of shoes! I thought about calling my CPA to see if I could write the expense off as a deduction—but decided he'd think I was crazy. Meanwhile, the clerk stood there looking bored. I fished out my credit card and he rang up the sale. As I left, he picked up his mobile phone and continued his conversation.

When I got home, I showed the shoes to my wife. She shook her head in dismay. "What are those things?" she asked, holding them as squeamishly as if they were a pair of dead rats. "They look awful."

"They're called running shoes. The clerk said they're the latest fashion."

"Have you lost your mind? Take them back!"

We discussed the matter for a while and finally decided to take a chance. If the granddaughter didn't like them, we could take them back. We mailed them to her, and about a week later got a "thank you" note from her. She adored the shoes. They were "awesome"—the envy of her neighborhood.

We live in a strange age. Often, doing the wrong thing turns out to be the right thing! Or vice versa! You just never know.

Blue Jean Blues

When I was a boy, there were three things I desperately hated: 1) squash 2) new shoes (they always hurt my feet for the first week) and 3) blue jeans. In those days I attended a country high school where everybody wore blue jeans. So I wore blue jeans too. But I despised them.

They were like torture devices—stiff, rigid, and abrasive. They felt, in fact, as if they were made of corrugated iron. The only possible way to put them on was to lie down on the floor and thrust your feet up into them. If you tried to sit in a chair while wearing them, your legs jutted out in front of you like stovepipes. If you tried to walk forward in a straight line, the jeans forced you to walk sideways. It was a happy day for me when I graduated from school and packed the jeans away forever.

But my escape was temporary. Blue jeans have made a comeback. In today's society, everybody wears them. Couples get married in them, President Bush and his cabinet wear them, and the Supreme Court justices probably wear them under their robes. My guess is that Pope Benedict XVI and Mother Angelica wear them after work.

But today's jeans are very different from the former variety. This was brought home to me recently by a display of them I saw in the window of a clothing store in the Mall. I was thunderstruck by their appearance. They looked like something the combatants had worn at the Battle of Gettysburg—tattered, torn, perforated, darned in places and so spattered with paint and motor oil that they resembled the canvases of Jackson Pollock. I entered the store and accosted one of the clerks.

"Excuse me," I said, "but those jeans in the window—are they secondhand?"

"Secondhand!" he cried angrily. "Are you trying to be insulting?"

"N…no," I sputtered. "I'm sorry. I didn't mean to upset you! But to tell the truth, they do look a bit secondhand."

He took a deep breath as if to calm himself down. "Sir," he said. "You are obviously laboring under a misapprehension. The garments you refer to as 'secondhand' are the very ultimate in style and fashion. They are known as 'Distressed Jeans' and are the creation of Pierre of Paris."

"Distressed Jeans!" I repeated in amazement. "Who would have thought it?"

"These jeans," he continued, "are the result of an elaborate process perfected after years of study. First, the jeans are mangled by robots until soft and pliable. Next, they are pulled through a series of enormous gears, which tear holes in them. After the holes are darned, the jeans are sprayed with paint by Pierre of Paris and shipped to America in hermetically sealed chests." He closed his ideas reverently. "They sell for $100 a pair."

"Gosh," I said. "I had no idea."

"Understandable in one of your age," he replied condescendingly.

As I left the Mall an idea occurred to me. In my attic at home was the box containing the jeans I had worn as a kid. They were tattered and torn, darned in places, and splashed with paint and grease. I had been planning to donate them to the Salvation Army—but now I realized I was sitting on a fortune. Why not hold a yard sale, label them "Distressed Jeans," and get $100 a pair for them? A bit unethical, maybe—but if Pierre of Paris could get by with it, why couldn't I?

Solo Shopping

My wife considers grocery shopping to be *her* job—and *hers* alone. She refuses to allow me any part in it. "Like all men, you're a failure as a shopper," she says. "You're a prey to impulse buying and phony bargains. If I were to let you do the shopping, we'd be broke in a month."

Occasionally, however, she drops the reins of command. Recently, as we parked outside the supermarket, she handed me her grocery list. "Do you think that you can go in the store and purchase these items without going wild?" she asked.

"I don't know what you mean by 'going wild!'" I retorted. "I'm actually a very conservative shopper. Somehow, you've managed to convince yourself that I become reckless when I get in a supermarket. Give me the necessary money, and I'll show you some *real* shopping."

"That's what I'm afraid of," she said, handing me a twenty-dollar bill. "Buy only the items on the list—and bring me the change. I'll take a nap while you're gone."

I went in the store whistling merrily. "I'll show her," I muttered to myself.

The first item on the list was *Salad Dressing*: "buy inexpensive store brand," she had scrawled. At the salad dressing counter I noticed a bottle of Caesar Salad. The price was a bit steep—$4.00—but what a salad it would make! I tossed it in the cart.

Next item on the list was "ground round." I looked over the selections at the meat counter, and a sign caught my eye: "T-Bone Steak. $10.00 a pound. Reduced for quick sale!" My wife approves of bargains—she'd be proud of me. I tossed a package of steak in the cart.

I glanced over the list: "peas—maybe Del Monte." How drab! Surely we could do better than that. I was passing the frozen food section at the moment, and I spotted a package that said: "Asparagus in Cheese Sauce."

Now there was real class for you! The price was $4.00—but so what? Just this once we'd splurge! I tossed it in the cart.

"Something for dessert," was the next item. Here was my chance to solo. At the bakery counter, I noticed a German rum cake plastered with white frosting and big red strawberries. Price: $10. I tossed it hastily in the cart, feeling the first pangs of guilt. My guilt increased at the checkout counter where the bill came to $32.79—with tax. I had to make up the difference out of my own pocket.

When I reached the car, my wife awoke from her nap. "How'd you make out?" she asked, stifling a yawn.

"Great!" I said, deciding to brave the thing out. "I upgraded the menu a bit."

She was now fully alert. "Give me the change!" she said anxiously.

"There was no change."

"No change! But there has to be change. Let me see the receipt."

She studied it and let out a little scream. "Thirty-two seventy-nine! Why, I could feed the Chinese army for that amount. You're a...you're a..." She groped for words. "You're a total failure as a shopper," she finished lamely.

"But think of the delicious supper we're going to have: Caesar Salad...T Bone steak...asparagus in cheese sauce...German rum cake..."

"None of the above," she muttered. "I just changed the menu."

"So what's it going to be now?" I asked.

"Crow!" she replied. "Cooked anyway you like. It's your call!"

Colds—Yesterday and Today

Despite the conquest of tuberculosis, meningitis, paralysis and hundreds of other life threatening diseases, medical science has been unable to conquer that simplest of all maladies—the common cold. Every year, millions of people all over the world go around with watery eyes and dripping noses, giving forth explosive sneezes that cause onlookers to scream "Gesundheit!" and run for cover. I don't quite understand this phenomenon. It's as though science isn't really trying.

I got to thinking about this recently and decided to help science correct this unfortunate situation by outlining various cold remedies that I have come across during my seventy-five years as a cold sufferer. I hope science appreciates my efforts.

1) The "Fight Cold with Cold" Theory. When I was a young man everybody believed in the homeopathic method of combating colds. According to this theory, you fought a disease by hitting back at it with the same conditions that caused it. Thus, if you had a cold you were advised to sleep in a freezing room without blankets and with all windows wide open. An ice cold bath or a dip in a chilly lake was prescribed, and the patient was urged to go out in the snow and chop a load of wood. This remedy often resulted in the patient getting pneumonia—but at least he got rid of the cold!

2) The "Give 'em Hell" Theory. As science advanced, the older theory gave place to the belief that a cold should be "sweated out." The patient was bundled into long underwear, placed in a tightly sealed room, and the heat turned up to its highest setting. Blankets and afghans were piled on—along with fur coats, quilts, rugs, foot warmers, and hot water bottles. When the patient was sweating profusely and screaming for mercy, he was forced to drink hot lemonade and steaming glasses of tea. This treatment was admittedly a "kill or cure" method—usually the former.

3) The "Gallon of Grog" Cure. This highly popular remedy required the patient to drink several quarts of pure bourbon, after which he became euphoric and fell into a deep sleep that sometimes lasted for a week. When he awoke, the cold was generally gone, but was replaced by the world's worst hangover.

4) The "Vitamin C" Cure. This theory, popularized by the late Dr. Linus Pauling, required the patient to dredge himself with vast quantities of orange juice and Vitamin C. The cure lost popularity when it was noted that the patient often swelled up like a huge naval orange and occasionally exploded.

5) The Herbal Cure. I swear by this remedy, having experienced its curative properties at first hand. Many years ago, I fell victim to a severe cold that refused to go away. A friend of mine referred me to a semi-retired doctor who had invented an infallible cold remedy. I located the old gentleman (who resembled Colonel Sanders) and he injected my arm with the contents of a large hypodermic needle.

"What's in that formula?" I asked.

He smiled, his eyes crossed briefly, and he said: "It's composed of allspice, basil, sage, oregano, marjoram, peppermint, and other secret herbs and spices"

When I returned home, my wife asked "What's that peculiar odor? You smell like a pumpkin pie." Dogs followed me around the neighborhood, and my fellow workers refused to let me in my office. This went on for about a week, after which the odor disappeared—as did the cold. I would gladly share this incredible secret with the medical world, but I have forgotten the doctor's name. A great loss to Science!

Deck the Halls with VISA and Master Cards

Back when I was a young lad, being in debt was a thing to be avoided at all costs (no oxymoron intended). Being in debt was like having hemorrhoids: you kept quiet about it and suffered in silence. If people knew you were in debt, they looked at you with the sort of pity reserved for tight rope walkers, lion tamers and deep sea divers—you were just an accident waiting to happen. Everybody wanted to be debt free, like the "Village Blacksmith" in Longfellow's famous poem. "He looked the whole world in the face and owed not any man."

But today things have changed. Today everybody is in debt up to their tonsils, and nobody seems to worry about it. In fact, people actually brag about it. If the Village Blacksmith were living today he would probably be looked on with suspicion. People would wonder if something was wrong with his credit rating.

A few days ago, for example, as I stopped by the bank, I saw a sleigh and six reindeer parked at the curb. A moment or two later, a fat little man with a white beard, red suit and high top boots skipped merrily out of the bank and climbed in the sleigh. He was mumbling "Ho! Ho! Ho!" and looking quite pleased with himself.

"Excuse me," I said timidly, "but aren't you…aren't you Santa Claus?"

"You got that right, bub. The fat old Elf himself. Although I must admit that I've shed a few pounds lately. Atkins Diet, you know!"

"Golly," I said. "This is amazing. But if you don't mind my asking: what were you doing in the bank?"

"Applying for a new line of credit," he said, with a merry twinkle in his eyes. "I've exceeded the limit on all my credit cards."

"Credit cards?" I said. "You mean you use credit cards?"

"Sure, doesn't everybody?" he replied. "I've got a wallet full of them: VISA, Master Card, Discovery Card…you name it, I've got it. And boy, how those totals add up! Would you believe I already owe over a million bucks?"

"Strange," I said. "I always figured you ran your business on a cash basis."

"What a quaint idea," he chortled. "Why operate on cash when you have good credit? Look at the government, for instance: trillion-dollar deficit and an eight trillion dollar national debt! But who worries? I understand Bush is planning to take out a Di Tech mortgage on the White House and put in an ATM Machine at Fort Knox."

"But how will you pay off all this credit card debt?"

"Who's talking about paying it off?" he asked, with a puzzled look. "As long as you keep up the monthly payments, everything's o.k. The banks love it!"

I shook my head in amazement. "But what about saving for a rainy day?"

"Saving? Watch your mouth, bub. That's a bad word these days." He picked up the reins of his sleigh. "Well, gotta go now. Gotta buy a new halogen headlight for my sleigh."

"But I thought Rudolph with his nose so bright guided your sleigh?"

"You're living in the past, bub. Rudolph got tired of the other reindeer laughing and calling him names, so he got a VISA Card and retired to Florida. As a matter of fact, I'm thinking of trading this old sleigh in on a jet plane—if my credit holds."

He cracked his whip and drove away, singing "It's beginning to look a lot like Christmas."

"Or like bankruptcy," I muttered as his sleigh disappeared from sight.

Getting to Know Your FBI Agent

Like lots of old timers, I am great admirer of the FBI. I hail from the good old days when the organization was as American as apple pie, Mother, baseball or a 401(k) Plan. In those days, if a crook learned that the FBI was after him, he would often go scurrying to the nearest FBI office and turn himself in. He knew he hadn't a chance.

Today, however, due to the success of terrorist groups, the FBI no longer commands the respect it once did. Comedians jeer at it, the public distrusts it, and I have even heard of cases where terrorists walk by its offices thumbing their noses and yelling "Yah, Yah! Can't catch me!"

Recently, in an effort to upgrade its tarnished image, the FBI adopted a new set of policies designed to anticipate terrorist threats. The agency plans to infiltrate the domestic scene in order to get to know the individual citizen better. In other words, the FBI will become more a part of your daily life—you'll get to know your FBI agent.

In line with this new plan, a pleasant young FBI agent called at my house a few days ago. "Hi, there," he said brightly, flashing his credentials. "I'm FBI agent Percy McClump. We're investigating your neighborhood, and I've been assigned to ask you a few personal questions. Hope you won't look on it as an invasion of your privacy. Remember: eternal freedom is the price of vigilance."

"I think you have that backwards," I chuckled, "but please come in. I'm a great admirer of your agency. J. Edgar Hoover is my hero. I know some people say he was a 'cross dresser'—but that's absurd. He was simply practicing 'disguise techniques.'"

As I ushered the agent in, I noticed a suspicious looking fellow slinking around my next-door neighbor's house. He wore a black cloak, a false beard and was studying the neighborhood with a pair of binoculars.

"Excuse me," I said, "but there's a man next door who's acting rather odd. He has a pair of binoculars and…"

"Not to worry," the agent assured me, taking out a note pad. "Probably just a bird watcher. O.K., let's start with the first question: have you ever worked for a terrorist group?"

"Not recently, "I answered. "I once worked for the Internal Revenue Service. But that guy next door…"

"Relax," he muttered. "He's probably just a pizza delivery man. Next question: do you keep any radio-active materials around your house?"

"A few bottles of Extra Hot Salsa Sauce," I replied. "But that man next door is unloading sacks of dynamite from his truck…"

"Probably going to remove some stumps from your neighbor's yard. Next question: Are there any deadly poisons around your house—such as might be used to infect a city's water supply?"

"Only a can of Draino," I said, "but it has one of those child proof caps that only a child can open. Look, I hate to keep a thing up, but that man next door…"

"Ha, ha!" he chuckled. "You certainly are the nervous type."

By this time, the man next door had taken shelter behind a large oak tree and had put his fingers to his ears.

"Last question: have you ever had any training as a crop duster?"

"No, but I had a high school course in Driver's Ed…as for that guy next door…"

"Naughty, naughty," he said. "You're not paying attention to my questions."

At that moment a loud explosion rocked the area, blowing my neighbor's house to pieces. The agent smiled and shook his head.

"Golly gee," he muttered. "Must have been a gas leak. I'll report it when I get back to the office." He shook my hand. "Meanwhile, let me thank you for your co-operation. If you notice anything unusual around your neighborhood, give us a call. Like I say: eternal freedom is the price of vigilance. And have a nice day!"

Dueling Boom Boxes

"Here it comes," the wife cried hysterically. "I can hear it in the distance. It's...it's like a nightmare!" We rushed to the window and gazed at the darkened street.

"Get the ear plugs ready!" I said unsteadily. "Nothing but ear plugs stand between us and insanity!"

The noise grew louder. It was like a tornado—or a herd of mammoths. I clutched my head in agony. The walls of the house trembled. We stared in horror as an SUV filled with screaming teen-agers sped by, their radio turned up full blast. The sound was deafening—a number by Metallica, I think. It reached a hideous crescendo and then died away. I glanced at my wife. She had fainted.

"Courage dear," I muttered. "I'll get you an aspirin."

"No," she screamed. "Straight Bourbon."

As we downed shots of Old Grandfather, we heard the thunderous approach of a second vehicle. We braced ourselves. Another SUV sped by, its radio blaring forth amplified strains of Jim Morrison's "Riders On the Storm."

"Can't the police do anything about this?" the wife asked in a trembling voice.

"No," I said. "They're helpless before this onslaught. We need..."

At that moment the beam of a searchlight filled the night sky, and the image of a huge bat appeared in the clouds. "It's the Police Chief calling Batman," I chortled. "Now we'll get some help."

Another SUV filled with howling teen-agers sped by, roaring out a Lynnrd Skynnrd number. Suddenly—out of nowhere it seemed—the familiar shape of the Batmobile appeared. The elderly figure of Batman (he's a Senior Citizen now, you know) could be seen driving the car.

But there was a second occupant in the Batmobile. Who could it be?

The vehicles raced along side by side, a radio in the Batmobile booming out strains of Beethoven's *Ninth Symphony*. The teen-agers screamed in pain, covered their ears with their fingers, and drove off in haste.

"We're saved," I cried. "The teen-agers can't stand classical music! It's driving them mad. A fitting revenge."

It was true. All night my wife and I watched as the familiar figure of Batman in his Batmobile chased teen-agers away with loud strains of Bach's *Brandenburg Concertos*, Wagner's *Ride of the Valkeries* and Tchaikovsky's 1812 *Overture*.

"Thank Heavens for Batman," my wife cried. "But there was another occupant in the Batmobile. Do you suppose it was Robin the Boy Wonder?"

"No," I replied. "Robin the Boy Wonder grew up during the age of the Beatles and the Rolling Stones. He loves Rock Music—has his own Rock Band. Batman couldn't stand it—forced Robin to leave Stately Wayne Manor."

"So who was in the car with Batman?" the wife asked.

"It was the Joker," I cried. "Like all Senior Citizens, he hates Rock Music. He and Batman have teamed up together to fight against it. Remember the old saying: 'The enemy of my enemy is my friend.'"

Asking Directions

I'm not a cynic. I believe most people are honest. If you ask them a question they will try to give you a truthful answer. But there are certain questions for which the temptation to lie is too great to be overcome. One such question is to ask someone for directions. I have never met a man who, if asked for directions, would admit that he did not know the answer. Historians tell us that even Abraham Lincoln could not be trusted in this matter. He would lie like everybody else.

The following true story will illustrate this strange phenomenon.

My wife and I had been invited by our friend George to attend his daughter's wedding in a little country town which I will refer to as Jonesville. We got on the Interstate and drove until we reached State Highway 27, where we turned off. There was a Chevron Station beside the road, and my wife suggested that I ask directions.

The clerk sitting behind the counter was a fat young man who wore a pair of purple shorts and a T Shirt that said, "Yale University." I hated to interrupt him because he was deeply engrossed in a copy of Marvel Comics.

"Excuse me," I said hesitantly, "I'm looking for directions to Jonesville?"

Reluctantly, he laid down the copy of Marvel Comics. "Jonesville?" he mumbled to himself. "Now let me see. Stay on Highway 27 fer about thirty miles 'till you come to Frog Legs Junction. Take a sharp right at the junction and drive 'till you see a store that sells handmade pottery. Turn left and go ten miles 'till you come to a busted windmill. Turn right, and you'll be on the road to Jonesville. You can't miss it."

I need hardly add that I missed it. Realizing that I was totally lost, I stopped at a dilapidated white building with a sign reading, "Whole Gospel Temple." A meeting of some kind was just letting out. I saw a grave looking old man wearing a black suit and hat and ambling along on a cane. "Howdy," I said, trying to sound folksy. "Sorry to trouble you, but can you give me directions to Jonesville?"

He pushed his hat back, scratched his wrinkled his brow. "Jonesville," he said. "Hmm. You done come too fur. Turn 'round, drive back 'bout twenty miles 'till you get to Possum Creek Road, take a sharp right and drive 'till you see a red barn with a sign on it says, 'Visit Look-Out Mountain.' Turn left and you'll be on the road to Jonesville. You can't miss it."

Once again, I managed to miss it. "That old man looked so honest," I said incredulously. "Why didn't he just admit he didn't know the way to Jonesville?"

"His pride was at stake," my wife replied. We drove on. Eventually, we came to a mailbox that said: "Harlow Biggs, Justice of the Peace."

"Now, we're getting somewhere," I said. "If you can't trust a Justice of the Peace, who can you trust?" I knocked at the door of the house, and a wrinkled old man appeared.

"Sorry to trouble you," I said, "but I'm trying to get to Jonesville."

"Jonesville," he repeated in a high nasal voice. "Lemme see, now. Drive straight on for thirty miles. You'll see a sign says 'Boiled Peanuts.' Take three left turns and you're on the road to Jonesville. You can't miss it."

I followed the old man' directions carefully. Half an hour later, my wife pointed out that something was wrong. "We've passed that same pig pen twice," she said.

"Old woodsman's trick," I assured her. "You go in circles until you double back on your original trail. Then you steer by the North Star."

Indeed, by this time the North Star was plainly visible in the sky. A few minutes later we heard the sound of traffic. "I hear cars—it must be the Interstate," my wife said. "And look—there's the Chevron Station where we started. What do we do now?"

"We go home," I said. "George has another daughter. When she gets married, we'll go to *her* wedding. And we'll take along a polygraph machine—just in case we have to ask for directions."

Gotta Keep Those
Pistons Pumping

I live in a neighborhood where everybody takes vigorous physical exercise. Each morning at dawn, the street in front of my house looks like an Olympic Trial Run. Young couples jog along with pained expressions on their faces, while middle-aged couples torture their bodies with something called "power walking." There are even a few octogenarians hobbling by on their canes. It's a glorious sight—but sometimes I wonder if all that energy could be put to better use.

An elderly neighbor of mine goes jogging each morning. I watch him through my picture window as I drink my morning coffee. He starts out energetically—like Rip Van Winkle doing the Macarena—but by the time he returns home he looks like a disabled aircraft making a crash landing.

I discussed the matter with him recently as he returned from one of his suicide missions.

"I recommend vigorous physical exercise for everybody," he said, coughing like a Gatling gun and turning blue in the face. "The body is a machine. You gotta keep those pistons pumping."

"But there are many kinds of exercise," I argued. "For instance, I do my own yard work. That's a form of exercise. I enjoy it."

"If you enjoy it, it probably isn't doing you much good," he said, nodding to a couple of octogenarians who limped by in agony. "Exercise has to be aerobic. You have to get your heart rate up."

"I've tried to get my heart rate up," I told him. "I timed it once after cutting the yard. It had dropped from 72 beats a minute to 65. Seemed to be going the wrong way."

"I get mine up to 80 beats a minute," he panted, as a bicyclist swerved to avoid hitting him. "Feel that pulse,"

I groped around on his wrist and found something that resembled a wet noodle having a panic attack.

"Just like a steam hammer," he said panted. "Gotta keep those pistons pumping."

By this time, the joggers had struggled home, the power walkers had given up and the octogenarians had crawled into their houses. The neighborhood was quiet.

Half an hour later, however, a new wave of activity had swept over the street. Lawn service trucks arrived, and workmen began unloading machinery. Soon the workmen were busy mowing grass, trimming hedges and scattering dust. The whine of leaf blowers and the howl of tractors filled the air. The men were sweating like ice pitchers.

But as I watched, I couldn't help feeling sorry for them. I suppose they thought they were getting plenty of exercise—but I knew they were just wasting their time. What they needed was real aerobic exercise, like jogging or power walking.

Gotta keep those pistons pumping.

How to Tell When You Are Getting Old

The following column is written for men. It is about how you can tell when you are growing old—a subject women are not interested in because, according to my wife, women do not grow old. They are like oak trees: they mature, they become statelier, they expand a bit—but they do not grow old. If you don't believe me, just ask the next woman you meet how old she is—and get ready to run.

But enough of this! I want to talk about the signs by which a man may know that he is getting old. Here are a few:

You try to get up from a couch, but have to rock back and forth several times to build up momentum.

Your hair goes out of business on your head but starts up a branch office in your ears.

You mention movie stars like Gene Autry, Myrna Loy, Spencer Tracy, Betty Davis or Johnny Weissmuller, and people give you puzzled looks.

You wonder why everyone seems to be talking in such low tones these days.

You say you are "feeling gay," and people around you start getting nervous.

You wonder why jar lids are tighter, suitcases weigh more, and stairs are built more steeply these days.

You start to tell a joke, forget the punch line—and your wife has to supply it for you.

You keep your old pair or glasses handy to help you find your new pair.

You ask your doctor how much time you have left, and he looks at his watch.

You wink at a pretty girl, and she asks if you have something in your eye.

You blow out the candles on your birthday cake and notice your wife standing behind you with an emergency oxygen tank.

You wonder why the local music store doesn't carry records by Lawrence Welk, Phil Spitalsky And His All Girl Orchestra or Spike Jones and His City Slickers.

Your granddaughter, who is writing a term paper on "The Battle of Gettysburg," calls you up and asks you for a first hand account.

The local funeral parlor keeps putting circulars under your windshield wiper.

At Christmas, when your house fills up with screaming grandchildren, you feel a strange new sympathy for Ebenezer Scrooge.

When you go jogging, you take along a book and a folding chair.

You go swimming, and the lifeguard gives you CPR *before* you enter the pool.

You decide to demonstrate to your grandchildren how to jitter-bug—and wake up in the ICU Unit of the hospital.

If any five of these signs apply to you, you may be getting old. If any ten apply to you, you should check your life insurance policy. If they all apply to you, you need to make an appointment with a good pathologist!

Sorry–I'm Away From My Desk

Did you ever get the feeling that you're living in a world from which human beings have disappeared and been replaced by machines? For instance, let's say you make a business call. What do you get? You get a menu. You dial one of the numbers on the menu. What do you get? You get a tape: "I'm sorry. Your party is away from his desk." This can go on all day. It's maddening—and frightening!

A few mornings ago, for instance, my bank statement came in the mail, and when I looked it over, I found an error. I immediately dialed the bank.

"Thank you for calling Banks a Million," said a recorded female voice. "This is Sondra Cartwheel, Information Secretary. I'm away from my desk at the moment on coffee break, but please listen to the following menu:

"If you have lost your VISA card and wish to speak with our janitor—Dial Extension 1. If you wish to report a bank robbery and know the culprit's name—Dial Extension 2. If you are applying for a loan—Dial Extension 3 (but don't get your hopes up.) If you just want someone to chat with, Dial Extension 4—Mr. Liverwurst, Director of Sprinkler Systems."

I decided to start with Mr. Liverwurst, so I dialed Extension 4 and listened to ten minutes of Tchaikovsky's *Overture to 1812*. As the music reached the point where Napoleon enters Moscow accompanied by church bells and canons, a high nasal voice came on the line: "You have reached the office of Reggie Liverwurst, Director of Sprinkler Systems. I'm away from my desk at the moment helping put out a fire at the Oak Street Branch, but if you will leave your name and number I'll call you back."

I left my name and number, had lunch, took a nap and called the bank again. I got the same menu, but this time I tried Extension 3—the loan department. "Good afternoon," said a sepulchral voice. "This is Roland Pecksniff, Director of Loans and Liens. I'm away from my desk at the moment chasing down a bad loan, but if you will leave your name and telephone number I'll call you back."

I was getting impatient now, but I dialed Extension 2. "Hi, there," said a brazen female voice that reminded me of my old army drill sergeant. "You have reached the office of Matilda Clophammer, Director of Security and Sanity. I'm away from my desk at the moment arresting a bank robber at our Maple Street Branch, but if you will leave your name and telephone number I'll call you back."

I dialed the last number on the menu—Extension 1. "Howdy, bub" said a creaky voice. "This here is Dusty Doolittle, custodian and hygienic specialist. I'm away from my desk getting a burger and fries, but if you'll leave your name and telephone number I'll call you rite back."

"That does it," I told my wife. "Nobody is ever at their desk anymore. How can we expect to survive as a nation? I'm going straight to the top about this problem."

I dialed the White House. "Hello," said a familiar voice. "This is President Bush. I'm away from my desk at the moment helping catch terrorists, but if you will leave your name and telephone number I'll return your call."

I sat back in my chair, my head spinning.

"What's wrong?" my wife asked. "You look bewildered."

"I *am*," I admitted. "I've been on the phone for two hours without talking to a single live human being. It's like that science fiction movie *The Body Snatchers*, or that Rapture thing the evangelicals are always talking about. I'm going out and knock on all the neighbors' doors to make sure there are still some *live* people out there. If anyone calls—tell them I'm away from my desk."

Golden Memories

On one of their recent visits, my grandchildren gathered around me and demanded a story. "Tell us about the Old Days," Lucy said. "You know—the time before they had television and bathrooms and microwave ovens and running water."

"Yeah," Mary Catherine chimed in, "like on the Flintstones."

It was time for my afternoon nap, and I was sleepy. "Grandpa doesn't feel like telling stories," I said. "See me after I take my nap."

"Please, Grandpa" they begged. "It doesn't have to be a good story—just a story."

"Oh, all right," I said reluctantly. "Give Grandpa a minute to think." I paused a few seconds trying to wake up, and then, in a dramatic voice, said: "It was the best of times; it was the worst of times…"

Lucy put a hand on her hip and shook her finger at me. "Grandpa," she said, "you didn't make that up. I saw it on a video. It was called *A Tale of Two Cities*."

"Perhaps you're right," I yawned. "Grandpa's memory is bad."

Lucy eyed me suspiciously. "All right," she said. "Go on with the story. But be sure it's your own composition."

"Well," I continued. "It was a long time ago—an era called the Depression."

"I know about depressions," Mary Catherine said. "I saw a program on NOVA called *Manic Depression*. All about women stabbing their husbands and stuff."

"No," I corrected gently. "This was a different kind of depression: a depression where everybody was poor. Nobody had any money."

"Why didn't they use their VISA cards?" Mary Catherine asked. "That's what Mama does when Daddy doesn't give her enough money."

"Times were hard," I continued, ignoring her. "One cold winter I had no coat to wear to school. So mama took a bundle of rags someone had given her, sewed them together and made me a coat of many colors. I wore it so proudly."

Both girls gave me skeptical looks. "Grandpa," Lucy said. "That was in a song by Dolly Parton. You stole it!"

"Borrowed it!" I corrected, my eyes closing sleepily. I could feel the bed calling me. "In those days there was no such thing as air conditioning. On hot summer nights we sat in the front yard waiting for the house to cool down. Sometimes a squad of mosquitoes would attack us. They were incredibly large. On one occasion, I saw my father fight off two of them with a Bowie Knife.

"Our meals were frugal," I continued. "Crusts of bread, skimmed milk, porridge. One day, father brought home some pork chops. It was the first meat I had ever tasted. Books were too expensive for us to buy, so I borrowed a copy of *Gray's Anatomy* from a friend. It rained that night, our roof leaked, and the book was ruined. I worked for two years splitting rails to earn money to replace the copy…"

"That sounds like Abraham Lincoln," Lucy said. "Teacher read us a book about him. Are you sure that really happened to you?"

"Certainly," I muttered groggily. "Then there was the time I flew a kite during a rain storm and proved that lightning and electricity are the same phenomenon. I became world famous…I wrote *Poor Richard's Almanac*…zzz."

I awoke with my daughter shaking me gently. "What on earth have you been telling the girls?" she asked. "They said you told them you were friends with Abraham Lincoln and that you invented electricity."

"You may fire when ready, Gridley!" I mumbled sleepily. "Four score and seven years ago. Fifty-four forty or fight…zzz."

Difficulties of an Elderly Babysitter

Being a grandfather these days is a tough job. Today's kids watch a lot of TV, study science in school, and keep up with the news. At an age when I was reading "See Jack Run," they know all about cholesterol, DNA, psychology, and the war in Iraq. Matching wits with them can be a humiliating experience, as I learned recently when I baby-sat my 8 year-old grandson, J. D., while my wife and daughter-in-law went shopping.

"How about Grandpa reads you some Mother Goose Rhymes?" I asked.

"Sure, Grandpa," J.D. replied. "But I've heard most of them. They're silly!"

Undaunted, I found an old copy of Mother Goose and thumbed through its brightly illustrated pages. "Here's an interesting one," I said. "Jack Spratt could eat no fat; his wife could eat no lean; and so between the two of them, they licked the platter clean."

J. D. gave me a puzzled look. "Why did Jack Spratt's wife eat such an unhealthy diet?" he asked. "She must have had high cholesterol. She should have been taking Lipitor."

"Hmm. Maybe she hadn't heard about it. Now here's one I think you'll like: 'Little Bo Peep has lost her sheep and doesn't know where to find them. Leave them alone and they will come home, wagging their tails behind them.' Look at the picture of Little Bo Peep crying because she can't find her sheep. Isn't that sad?"

"Not really," he said, studying the picture carefully. "If she's lost her sheep she can always clone some new ones. All she needs is some DNA from one of the old sheep. They did it with Dolly."

"Maybe you're right," I said, turning to another poem. "How about this one: 'Jack be nimble; Jack be quick; Jack jump over the candle stick.' Isn't that cute?"

"It's sort of weird!" he said. "Why did the poor kid keep jumping over the candle stick like that? Sounds like he had Attention Deficit Disorder. Maybe some Ritalin would have calmed him down."

"Hmm. Let's try this one: 'Humpty Dumpty sat on a wall; Humpty Dumpty had a great fall; All the king's horses and all the king's men, couldn't put Humpty together again,' Now what do you think of that?"

"I think the king's men needed a course in emergency medical procedure. They should have given him CPR, kept him warm, and phoned 911."

"Er...yes," I said, putting the book aside. "Maybe these poems *are* a bit young for you. I'll tell you some stories. Do you know the one about Ali Baba and the Forty Thieves?"

"Yeah, but I'd rather hear about Osama bin Laden and the Taliban. He lives in a cave like the 40 thieves, and there's a $25 million reward for him."

"Hmm. Have you heard 'Goldilocks and the Three Bears?'"

"No, but it sounds good. Like something on the Discovery Channel."

I told the story with great animation. He listened attentively—but with increasing bewilderment.

"Did you like that one?" I asked hopefully.

"Yeah, but I didn't get that part about Goldilocks busting into the Three Bears' house. That's known as 'breaking and entering.' Even bears have civil rights."

"I hadn't thought of that," I said. "I know: I'll tell you 'Little Red Riding Hood.'"

Just at that moment my wife and daughter-in-law came back from shopping. "How'd it go?" my daughter-in-law asked, putting down her packages.

"O.K." I replied. "But I'm glad you came home when you did. I was just about to tell J. D. the story of Little Red Riding Hood, and I was dreading the part where the wolf dresses up in Grandma's nightgown."

"Why should that bother you?"

"I was afraid J. D. would start asking if the wolf was a cross-dresser."

Finding Yourself:
The New Hobby

These days young people are having a lot of trouble "finding themselves." I'm not sure what "finding yourself" means, but I do know it's important Until young people "find themselves" life is scarcely worth living.

I was discussing this subject recently with a friend of mine whose kids, like mine, are having trouble "finding themselves." We share the same perplexities.

"How's your son doing these days?" I asked. "Still trying to find himself?"

"Yeah," he answered wearily. "Two months ago he called us from New Zealand. He said he was working for an international group called STDBP—Save the Duck-Billed Platypus. Last week he called us from Tibet. He was living in a monastery in the Himalayas, tending a herd of yak and learning to play the sitar. I hope he'll hurry and 'find himself' before I go broke paying his travel expenses."

"I know what you mean," I said. "One of my kids is in Kyoto, Japan waiting tables in a Sushi restaurant. Another has joined an expedition to Canada in search of Big Foot."

My friend nodded. "It was different when you and I were young. My dad gave me the Help Wanted section of the newspaper, a quarter for carfare, and told me to find a job. That's how we 'found ourselves' in those days."

Later that day a student at the college where I teach came up after class. He had the typical college look: green dyed hair, metal rings in his eyebrows and a T-shirt that said "Protect Wild Life in Botswana and Neighboring Areas."

"Excuse me, professor," he said. "I'm in the process of 'finding myself,' and I need your help. My yoga master said to consult 'those who are wiser than I.'"

"Thanks for the compliment. What seems to be the problem?"

"Basically, I can't decide whether to go to the Australian Outback and become a sheep herder or go to Sri Lanka and become a pearl diver."

After thinking the matter over, I said: "Well, when I was a young guy and couldn't make up my mind about something, I'd just flip a coin."

He gave me a long, penetrating stare. "That's awesome!" he said. "Wait until I tell my yoga master. I'm eternally grateful to you."

At lunch time I decided to grab quick bite at McDonalds. As I entered the Drive Through lane and stopped to give my order, I heard what sounded like a sigh coming from the microphone. Then a girl's voice said, "Your order, please."

"A cheeseburger and coke. And excuse me for sticking my nose in your business, but I couldn't help hearing you sigh just now. You don't sound happy."

"I'm not," she said, "and it's all because I can't…"

"Can't find yourself," I suggested.

"I'm seeking my identify—trying to find my own living space." At that moment the cars behind me began honking, so I had to drive on. I felt sorry for the poor kid.

When I returned home that afternoon, my wife asked, "How was your day?"

"All right, I guess. But I'm a bit puzzled. It suddenly dawned on me that I haven't 'found myself.' When I was growing up, I never had the time. I never journeyed to Sri Lanka, learned to play the sitar or eat Sushi."

"Well, it's too late now," she said unsympathetically. "If you tried it at your age you'd probably have a heart attack—or get thrown in the bug house."

"I guess you're right," I replied, sinking into my easy chair and switching to the movie channel. "I'm too old. Sad, isn't it? But there are compensations. 'Not finding yourself' is a lot more comfortable—and a lot cheaper."

The Case of the Disappearing Socks

Psychologists have had plenty to say about "sex problems" in marriage. What they have failed to consider, however, is the equally important "socks problem."

Ann Landers and Dear Abby seem unaware of it. Carl Jung and Sigmund Freud never mentioned it.

But I would be willing to bet that it has broken up more marriages than all the sexy blond secretaries in the world.

Let me explain. In the chest of drawers in our bedroom there is a drawer which I call the "unmatched sock drawer." It contains an accumulation of all my odd socks that have lost their mates through the years.

Recently, I made a count of these unmatched socks; there were 27 of them. Time for the ritual "socks fight."

I called my wife into the bedroom and told her the results of my count. Immediately, I could see her going into her "damage control mode."

"I hope you're not implying that I lost the mates to those socks," she said.

"Well, if you didn't, then who did?"

"I haven't the least idea!"

"You haven't the least idea!" I said sarcastically. "All right. Let's take it by the numbers. Who washes my sock?"

"I do, of course, but that doesn't mean I lost the missing ones."

"Look," I said in a cool, logical voice, "let's use an analogy. Suppose you are a teller in a bank. At the end of the day, the bank manager counts the money in your drawer and discovers that you're $27 short. Who does he blame? Obviously, he blames you."

"That's the stupidest analogy I ever heard," she replied. "If I'm a teller at a bank and money is missing from my drawer, it suggests that I stole it. But if your socks are missing, does it suggest that I stole them? Of course not! Why would I want to steal your old socks? In my opinion, they're extremely ugly."

'You're…you're being illogical," I said, realizing there was a flaw somewhere in her argument but not being able to find it.

"I think I'm being quite logical, thank you! Besides, if you would let me buy some decent looking socks for you, this wouldn't be happening." She pointed to a green sock ornamented with bulbous yellow triangles. "That one looks like a sick frog. And look at this one with the hole in the toe. Why should I worry myself about something that ought to be given to the Salvation Army?"

"You're trying to change the subject. As of right now there are 27 unmatched socks in my drawer. How would you feel of 27 of your silk stockings were missing."

"I don't wear silk stockings. I wear panty hose. Most women do."

Of course, she had the last word. "Next time I get married," she said, flinging herself out of the room, "I'm going to marry a one-legged man!"

The Strange Hobby of
Coupon Clipping

It was Sunday morning.

I lit my pipe, went out on the lawn and brought in the oversized newspaper. Laying its unwieldy bulk on the kitchen table, I glanced cautiously around to make sure my wife wasn't watching. Then, I removed a large mass of ads from inside the paper and carried them over to the wastebasket.

I'm an obsessive "thrower outer"—I hate clutter. My wife, on the other hand, is an obsessive "coupon clipper." She scatters the newspaper ads around her and whacks away at the coupons—a veritable Jack the Ripper.

I was holding a large package of ads poised above the waste bin when my wife unexpectedly entered the room.

"Stop!" she screamed. "Don't you dare throw those ads out until I've gone through them." She left the room and returned brandishing a pair of scissors.

"You know I love to clip coupons," she said, giving me a dirty look.

"Sheer waste of time," I commented.

"That just shows how little you know," she replied, holding up a coupon for me to see. "Look at this: if you buy three boxes of tapioca pudding and mail in the coupon, they'll send you a 50-cent refund. How about that, Mr. Smarty!"

"So?" I said. "First, I don't like tapioca pudding. It reminds me of fish eggs. Second, the stamp costs 39 cents. Total profit: 11 cents. Big deal!"

"It all adds up," she said. "Here's one you'll have to admit is a bargain. Buy three boxes of Fluffy Duffy, mail in the coupon, and they'll send you a free box."

"But what, exactly, is Fluffy Duffy?"

"I'm not sure," she admitted. "I think it reduces static cling."

"Static cling!" I said sarcastically. "That's got to be the world's smallest problem. As a matter of fact, I find static cling rather interesting."

She paid no attention. "Listen to this," she gloated. "Buy $40 worth of groceries every week for 16 weeks, present this coupon, and the store will give you a free ham."

"Sixteen weeks!" I sneered. "That's four months. I doubt if I'll even be around in four months."

"Where are you going?"

"I'll probably die of bird flu or something."

"Then I'll eat the ham myself," she retorted.

"I tell you what I think," I said, relighting my pipe and striding about the room. "I think the manufacturers are playing games with you. They're operating a 'clip joint'—if you'll pardon the pun. Why not just reduce the price of the article?"

"People wouldn't buy it," she replied.

"Then they didn't need it in the first place," I said, puffing on my pipe.

A few minutes later she gave me a look of triumph. "Well, I may just as well throw this one away," she said, holding up a coupon. I glanced at it hastily—and then read it more carefully. It was a coupon allowing $2 off on a large can of Sir Walter Raleigh—my favorite brand of tobacco.

"Hmm," I muttered, "Looks pretty good. I'll make an exception this one time. Give me the coupon."

"First, admit that you were wrong."

"But I wasn't wrong. This is just the exception that proves the rule."

"No admission—no coupon," she gloated.

I hesitated a moment. "All right," I said grudgingly. "I was wrong—to some degree."

"And promise not to take it back later?"

"Of course I won't take it back later. I'm a man of my word."

Little did she know that I had my fingers crossed behind my back After all, a man has to have some way to salvage his pride.

The Art of Dieting

My friends ask me how I manage to stay so trim. I am five foot eleven inches tall, weigh two hundred and forty-five pounds, wear extra large underwear and size forty-six pants. Not bad for an old guy, I'd say. (My doctor, who is a bit of a fanatic, says I'm overweight—but I ignore him. These modern weight tables are all wrong.)

How do I do it? I stick to a diet of eighteen hundred calories, drink plenty of liquids (three beers a day) and exercise sensibly by walking to the mailbox and back.

I must admit that I could not maintain this puritanical regimen without my beloved wife. When I'm around food, she watches over me like a hawk, and at parties has been known to snatch a delicacy from my hand. What a woman!

Let me illustrate my method of weight control by describing one of our recent forays to the grocery store. We shop at a large super market known as Banjos. As we enter its portals, I usually experience one of my "weak spells." I have a condition known as hypoglycemia, or "low blood sugar." When it strikes, I need instant nutrition.

"I'm having an attack of hypoglycemia," I cry, turning deathly pale.

"Very well," the wife sniffs, "eat an apple."

In desperation, I purchase a Milky Way candy bar and scarf it down. To make sure my blood sugar is at the right level, I force myself to eat a second Milky Way.

We approach the vegetable and fruit display. "I think I'll buy some broccoli for supper," the wife says. "Wait here until I come back."

"Certainly," I reply, refreshing myself with a third Milky Way bar that I have carefully concealed in my pocket

While waiting, I notice a young lady offering free samples of strawberries dipped in chocolate. "Yes, I'll have one," I say, making sure my wife isn't watching. "In fact, I'll have two: one for me, one for my wife."

Remembering that my wife doesn't care for strawberries, I eat both. We move on to the next aisle. While my wife is buying a package of rice, I sample a link of pork sausage that a sales lady is distributing.

Next, we pass the frozen food display. As my wife walks ahead, I bolt down a slice of pepperoni pizza that a salesman is handing out. It strengthens my blood sugar so much that I ask for another—and he graciously complies.

Our next stop is the dairy counter. As my wife picks over the milk, I notice an attractive salesgirl offering samples of roquefort cheese on Ritz crackers. "Delicious!" I cry, bolting one down.

"Care for seconds?" the girl asks pleasantly.

"Since you insist—yes!"

At the meat counter—while my wife chats with the butcher—I munch a slice of frankfurter, gobble down a wedge of barbecued beef, and enjoy a chunk of hot pastrami. They're so generous with those free samples!

As we are making our way through the checkout booth, a saleslady offers me a twist of beef jerky. Since my wife is too busy paying the check to notice, I accept gratefully.

At supper that night, my wife serves skinless chicken, broccoli, and rice. "You did well today," she says. "With me to watch over you, you eat a very healthy diet."

"Yes," I reply, "but you have to give *me* a little credit for will power."

Not Letting Terrorists
Spoil Your Fun

The President and the authorities are all saying the same thing: don't let the threat of Terrorism disrupt your normal way of life. Don't let Terrorists spoil your fun!

A few days ago, my wife remarked: "I'd like to shop for some curtains in the Mall, but I'm worried about a Terrorist attack."

"Nonsense," I replied. "Don't you read the papers? The authorities tell us not to let Terrorists spoil our fun."

My wife glanced through the window.

"There are three men in turbans and white robes gathered around our car," she said in a frightened voice. "They've opened the hood and are placing some kind of device on the motor. Shouldn't you investigate?"

"Not to worry," I said, yawning. "They're probably just pizza delivery men."

At that moment there was a loud explosion outside. "The car just blew up," my wife said hysterically.

"Relax," I told her, smiling calmly. "Remember what the authorities say: don't let Terrorists spoil your fun. We'll take the bus to the Mall."

When we reached the Mall, we made our way through bustling throngs of people until we reached the Acme Department Store where my wife wanted to look at curtains. As we entered the store, we heard machine gun fire. "What's happening?" I asked a clerk who was cowering behind a counter.

"The FBI is shooting it out with a gang of Terrorists," she replied.

"Shouldn't we leave?" my wife asked. "I'm frightened."

"And let Terrorists spoil our fun? Forget it. Where is your curtain department, young lady?" I asked the clerk.

"Two aisles down and turn left," she replied, as a grenade exploded overhead.

When we reached the curtain department, a clerk's head emerged from beneath the counter. "May I...may I help you?" she stuttered.

"I'm looking for something in white satin," my wife replied, as a chandelier exploded overhead. "These look nice," she added hastily. "I'll take them."

"VISA or Master Card?" the clerk asked, lifting a hand above the counter.

"VISA," I replied, ducking down to avoid a shower of bullets,

As we left the store and walked through the Mall, my wife said: "Don't you think we should go home? This is making me nervous."

"You're playing right into the hands of the Terrorists," I replied. "We're mustn't let them spoil our fun. Here's a McDonald's Restaurant. Let's get a hamburger."

We entered the restaurant. "Two Cokes and a two Big Macs," I told the clerk.

"I wouldn't advise the Big Macs, sir," she said. "A terrorist poured anthrax in the hamburger meat. How about some Chicken McNuggets instead?"

We took our order to a table and sat down. I gave a contented sigh. "Isn't this pleasant?" I murmured. "I'm not letting a bunch of Terrorists spoil my fun."

At that moment, I noticed a television set placed over the doorway of the restaurant. It was tuned to the financial channel. I glanced at it, and choked on my drink.

"What's wrong?" my wife asked.

"The market is down four hundred points," I cried hysterically, leaping up from my seat. "I've got to get home and call my broker."

"But the authorities said we shouldn't let Terrorists spoil our fun."

"Yes" I cried, rushing toward the exit, "But they didn't tell us what to do during a BEAR attack!"

A Trip to Oz

When you get my age, it's the little things in life that please: taking a long nap on the couch while your wife does the dinner dishes, turning off a commercial you hate, tip-toeing to your room and locking the door when the grandchildren get too noisy…

Yes, these are indeed the things that make life worthwhile. But nothing can compare with the simple joy of a Walk Through the Mall on a Saturday Night. It's cheap, pleasant, and, for an old guy like me, as exciting as climbing Mt. Everest.

My wife and I always begin our walk by having dinner in the Mall cafeteria. I make the usual resolutions to eat "just a bite;" but those clever cafeteria folk know how to break your will: "Yes, I'll have the small mixed salad without any dressing—no, wait—the shrimp and avocado salad looks better…yes, the blue cheese dressing, please…and a bowl of gumbo…and a slice of roast beef…and fried potatoes and…No, I better skip dessert…Oh well, what harm can a slice of coconut pie do?…And a couple of rolls with butter…and coffee with cream and sugar…"

Leaving the cafeteria like a cargo ship that has just taken on ballast, I lead the wife through crowds of shrieking teen-agers, squalling babies, gray haired old geezers, fat ladies, skinny ladies, and seductive blondes and brunettes.

"Stop looking at that girl," the wife says. "What's that you say? She's a decided blonde, is she? You're right about that—she *decided* to be a blonde. Look where you're going or you'll fall and break a hip. And don't even think about the Cookie Store!"

We stroll past kiosks selling picture frames, silver jewelry, Mickey Mouse watches, and grains of rice with the Declaration of Independence stamped on them.

A Mid-Easterner at one of the kiosks stops us. "You maybe like a solid silver champagne bucket, sir? Only five bucks. Jus' zee sing for your next birthday."

"No thanks, young man. I'm not sure I'll even make it to my next birthday."

We approach a display of shiny new automobiles. "Care to take a chance on a Jaguar, sir?" a dapper young clerk asks. "Radar controlled brakes, digital computer, plutonium gears, leopard skin seat covers, automatic ice-maker: two bucks a chance!"

The wife gives my arm a jerk. "You couldn't drive the thing if you won it! You have enough trouble steering our old 1990 Toyota. Come on."

As we pass *Victoria's Secret*, I glance at the mannequins in the window.

"Stop looking at those unclad mannequins," the wife says sharply. "They could be used in a medical text book."

"I was trying to figure out Victoria's Secret," I reply with offended dignity.

"Even the CIA can't figure that out," the wife says. "Wait here. I'm going in *Toys R Us* to buy little Lucy her birthday present. And don't go near that cookie store."

"Hmm," I mutter, as she leaves. "No harm in *looking* at the Cookie Store. Umm, those frosted caramels are tempting...Steady on, old man, you've had enough dinner to kill a Tyrannosaurus Rex...On the other hand, you only live once...Yes, miss, three of the frosted caramels and two of the vanilla creams—No, wait—cancel that order...No, dear, of course I didn't buy any cookies..."

Like I say: it's the little things that make life worthwhile!

Gathering Moss With the Rolling Stones

A few months ago at a local music store I bought my son a CD for his birthday. As I handed the clerk my credit card, she asked me if I wanted to sign up for a free copy of *Rolling Stones Magazine*. She assured me that it was just a promotion, and that I wouldn't be subscribing to the magazine. "In case anything goes wrong," she added, "you can call this number." She wrote it on a piece of paper.

A month later a copy of the magazine arrived. A picture on the cover showed a group of wrinkled, gray haired men, banging away on guitars in the frenzied style of the 60's.

I showed the magazine to my son. "Who are those old guys?" I asked. "They look like escapees from a concentration camp."

"Don't you recognize them, Dad? That's Mick Jagger and Keith Richards, *The Rolling Stones*. They're making their final tour."

"Thank heaven for small blessings!" I cried.

"I know how you hate rock music," he said. "Why did you subscribe to the magazine?"

"I didn't subscribe. The clerk at the music store said it was just a free one-time promotion. I thought you might like it."

"Hmm," he said, looking at the cover. "Your name and address are on the label. I think they've tricked you into subscribing. You better call them up and get things straightened out."

I looked up the number the clerk had given me, dialed it, and after a long wait, heard a high pitched voice speaking in slightly broken English.

"Hello to you. This Magazine Clearing House Bureau. My name Kim Yang. How I help you, please?"

I've faced this situation before. It's called "out-sourcing." These days, in an effort to cut costs, many companies are routing telephone calls to agents in foreign countries. Unfortunately, some of the agents don't speak very good English.

"Hello to you, Mr. Yang," I said, unconsciously falling into his speech pattern. "I happy talk with you."

"Thank you," he said politely. "I happy talk with *you*."

I realize I should have gotten right down to business, but something about Mr. Yang intrigued me. "What country you speekee from?" I asked conversationally.

"I speakee from South Korea" he answered brightly.

"Ah so!" I said. "That very good country. I likee that country very much."

"Thank you!" he said. "I likee *your* country velly much."

Having gotten diplomatic relations off to a good start, we moved on to business.

"You wishee help with problem?" he asked.

"Yes," I said, "I wishee help with problem."

"What is problem, please?"

"Some days ago, I subscribe to magazine. When magazine come, I find I no likee magazine."

Mr. Yang paused thoughtfully. "Why you no likee magazine?"

"Magazine for young man," I said. "I old man."

He thought this over. "You wishee magazine for old man?"

"No," I said. "I not wishee magazine for old man."

Another long pause. "Old lady?"

"No," I said. "Not old lady."

"Young lady?"

"No," I said rather loudly. "Not any lady!"

Another long pause. "You not likee *any* lady?"

"I likee *some* lady," I replied. "That not my problem. My problem: I wishee cancel subscription to magazine."

"Oh, ho!" he said joyfully, like the Buddha achieving enlightenment. "Why you not say so? That velly simple matter. I fix."

"Thank you very much," I said.

"Thank *you* velly much," he responded. "What name, please?"

"*Rolling Stones!*" I said.

"That your first name or last name?"

"That not my name at all," I said. "*Rolling Stones* name of magazine."

"*Wolling Stones*," he repeated slowly. "That velly strange name. I not find *Wolling Stones* in magazine list."

"You lookee in R's?" I asked.

"No. I lookee in W's."

"You must lookee in R's."

"Excuse, please. I am thinking *Wolling* begin with W."

"No," I insisted. "Wolling...I mean Rolling...begin with R."

"Hmm," he said. "Velly strange."

"Not so strange. Chinese people have trouble to say 'R' Make it sound like 'W.'"

"Ah, so!" he said. "But I not Chinese person. I South Korean person."

"Yes, I know," I replied. "And South Korea very good country."

"Thank you. Your country also velly good country."

We were right back where we started. "I must go now, Mr. Yang. I call back later. Thank you very much."

"Thank you velly much," he said.

I called back the following week and got an agent whose English was considerably better than Mr. Yang's. He understood my problem immediately and cancelled my subscription. He was very business-like and efficient. He even pronounced his 'R's' correctly. But he wasn't half as much fun as Mr. Yang.

A Readers Digest
History of Mobile

There are many excellent histories of Mobile, Alabama in our local book-stores, notably those by Jay Higgenbotham and Caldwell DeLaney. The problem, however, is that most of them are a bit long. Some of them take weeks to read (even months if you're a slow reader), and in the meantime, your bills go unpaid, the dog needs walking, the garbage piles up and your wife starts yelling at you. So, in an attempt to solve this problem, I got out my old Remington Rand typewriter, bought a new ribbon from Best Buy and wrote the following concise history of our city.

Of course, I'm not a professional historian and have done very little research. In fact I haven't done any at all—so some of the facts may be wrong. But so what? That never bothered politicians, lawyers, or people at cocktail parties. If you come across a fact you don't like, read on until you find one you like better. There are enough to go around.

◆　　　◆　　　◆

Mobile was founded in 1307 by a tribe of Indians known as the Maubelas or Ma Bells (they took their name from the well known tele-phone company). They had hiked down from Atmore to do a little sun bathing on the Gulf Coast, but when they reached Mobile they aban-doned their plans because it was raining. They waited several years for the rain to stop, and when it didn't, they imported a Medicine Man (the equivalent of today's weather man). He promised them that the rain would stop by the weekend, but, like all weathermen, he got it wrong. So the Indians scalped him, built a huge structure known as the Convention Teepee and started the first Miss Junior Squaw Contest.

The years passed, and in 1407 a real estate speculator named DeSoto came over from France to buy property on the Gulf Coast before prices started going up. When he reached Dauphin Island, however, he discovered he was too late—all the teepees had "For Sale" signs on them, and the Indians were making a fortune in real estate. Undeterred, De Soto pushed westward, discovered the Mississippi River, (which he named "The Mississippi River") and died of the first case of Mad Oyster Disease.

O.K. A few centuries went by and, in the year 1712, two brothers—Sieur d'Bienville and Sieur d'Iberville—came over from France and founded Mobile, which they named after the well-known gasoline company. Since both brothers were named "Sieur," their names caused a lot of confusion. Somebody would yell, "Can you come here a minute, Sieur?" and both brothers would come running. A fistfight would usually ensue and both brothers would end up in jail. So to stop the confusion, Sieur d'Iberville pushed westward, discovered New Orleans (which he named "New Orleans"), and died from Mad Oyster Disease.

Meanwhile, the other brother (the one named Sieur d'Bienville) had a colorful history. He hung around Mobile for a while, built the city's first drainage system (which has been flooding regularly ever since) and died from Mad Oyster Disease (the French are particularly prone to this malady).

In his honor, Mobilians built an eight-sided park in the center of town and named it Bienville Octagon. Through the years, people ignored the "Keep Off the Grass" signs, took short cuts through the park, and wore the sides down—which is why the park is known today as Bienville Square.

(Next time—The Beginning of Mardi Gras—and stuff like that!)

A Reader's Digest History of Mobile (2)

Let's see—where was I? Oh, yes, at our last meeting, I was explaining the origin of Bienville Octagon—or Bienville Square, as it is known today. As the years passed, Mobile became a large city. First it belonged to the French, then to the Spanish, then to the English and then to the Americans. It was shuffled back and forth like a ping-pong ball. Apparently nobody wanted it. This gave the inhabitants an inferiority complex. Some turned to drink, some to psychoanalysis, some to sports, and still others to art. Finally, they all turned back to drink.

A depression swept the city—which was fortunate, since the place hadn't been swept for years. In an attempt to cheer people up, the City Fathers instituted a holiday known as Mardi Gras. The name means Fat Tuesday. The holiday was originally called Fat Monday—but the Postal Workers changed it to Fat Tuesday so they could have a four day weekend.

The holiday proved to be a great success. Gigantic floats rolled down the streets, creating huge pot holes—which the City Fathers have kept to this day as a memorial to by-gone times. There was revelry, music, dancing and the consumption of Moon Pies, a delicacy that served as both food and weapons of mass destruction.

Mardi Gras ended when the Civil War broke out. Historians tell us that the war was based on a mistake. General P. T. Beauregard, (nick-named "The Ragin' Cajun") attended a party in Charleston one night, got drunk and began firing his pistol at Fort Sumpter. By the time his friends got the pistol away from him, the war had started.

The war created great confusion. At first, the South seemed to be winning, then the North, then the South again. At half time, the score was tied. During the ensuing struggle, Admiral Faragut sailed into Mobile Bay, yelling, "Damn the mosquitoes—full speed ahead!" He was fined for using profanity in public.

Meanwhile, Admiral Raphael Semmes, Mobile's naval hero, captured the entire Union Navy but released them when they convinced him that they were a fleet of Carnival Cruise ships. Today, Semmes' statue stands at the foot of Government Street. It is painted green in memory of the attacks of seasickness that he often experienced.

It was at this time that Madame Octavia Le Vert became famous as Mobile's most notable Blue Stocking (nylons were hard to obtain during the War). One night, three escaped Union Soldiers broke into her bedroom, and, in a fit of generosity, she hid them under her bed. Unfortunately, there were already three Confederate soldiers hiding under her bed. A big fight broke out, immortalized by Father Patrick Ryan (the Poet of the Confederacy) in a poem titled "The Battle Hymn of the Republicans."

The war ended when General Lee and General Grant met at Appomattox Court House for a game of poker. Grant, who had been drinking and was in one of his silly moods, stole Lee's sword and refused to give it back unless Lee promised to surrender. So Lee, who was too much of a gentleman to spoil a joke, surrendered.

The end of the war brought many changes to Mobile. A new class of entrepreneurs arose and made vast fortunes in lumber, cotton, Krystal hamburgers and moon pies. Known as the Bourbon Generation in honor of their favorite beverage, they built the beautiful mansions, which today line Government Street, including McDonalds Restaurant, Popeyes Fried Chicken, and Taco Bell.

(Editors note: Mr. Varnado will continue his history if he can raise enough money to pay his bail. Small contributions gratefully received—larger in proportion.)

A Channel For All Seasons

Just as I'm sitting down to supper, the phone rings.

"Excuse me, sir," says a pleasant female voice. "I'm calling from your local TV Cable Company. We'd like to tell you about a new cable TV package we're offering. It contains fifty new and exciting channels and is yours for only $75 a month."

"Thank you miss, but we already get enough channels to satisfy the most ardent Couch Potato. We get the Disney Channel, the Weather Channel, the Gourmet Channel, the Nature Channel, the Romance Channel, the Mystery Channel…"

"May I ask your age, sir?"

"If it's any of your business, I'm seventy-three."

"Congratulations, and long may your arteries remain unclogged! At your advanced age I know you'll be interested in our new Gerontology Channel, which features such exciting shows as 'The Stroke Doctor,' 'Paralysis Anybody?' 'Conquering Your Constipation,'—plus two new soap operas: 'The Old and the Bedridden,' and 'All My Great Grandchildren.'"

"Sounds interesting, young lady, but…"

"And I know our Games Channel will interest you. It provides a line-up that includes such super shows as 'Hop Scotch For the Millions,' 'Better Bungy Jumping,' 'Darts For Dummies,' 'Water Polo Anybody?'"

"I'm afraid I'm not much of a games person…"

"More sedentary type, eh? Then how about our Sleep Channel? You'll revel in such favorites as 'The Evening Snooze Hour' with Jim Lehrer,' 'I Married a Sleep Walker,' 'Saturday Night Dead…'"

"I don't believe…"

"Or perhaps you'd prefer our Dentistry Channel, which brings you shows like 'Tooth or Consequences,' and movies like 'The Bridges of Madison County,' 'Root Canal Diary,' 'God's Little Achers...'"

"I'm afraid I wouldn't..."

"And I know you'll go wild over our Eskimo Channel with a line-up that includes 'This Old Igloo,' 'Grooming Your Polar Bear,' and..."

"To tell you the truth, young lady, we don't watch much T.V. Except for the news, we don't care for most shows and..."

"I understand perfectly. That's why the package includes our 'T.V. For Folks Who Hate T.V' Channel. Twenty-four hours of totally blank screen, without any commercial interruptions..."

"Thanks, young lady, but..."

"And there's also our Assisted Suicide Channel, with a twenty-four hour hotline answered personally by Dr. Kevorkian...or..."

"I'm afraid I'm not..."

"And we mustn't forget the Komodo Dragon Channel...the German Measles Channel...The Manic Depressive Channel...the Trombone Channel...the Alcoholics Anonymous Channel......"

"I have an appointment, Miss..."

"...the Monster Truck Channel...the Aardvark Channel...the Steam Fitters Channel...the Tse Tse Fly Channel...the Tax Cheater's Channel...the Dork Channel...

CLICK!

The Passing of Old Adages

When I was a kid, people were constantly bombarding me with annoying adages that made my life miserable. For instance, if I was reading a book late at night and didn't want go to bed, somebody was sure to say: "Early to bed, early to rise, makes a man healthy, wealthy and wise." If I procrastinated over my homework, I would be told: "Never put off until tomorrow what you can do today." There seemed to be an adage lurking around every corner, ready to leap out at me.

Benjamin Franklin was responsible for most of these adages, and history tells us he didn't do a particularly good job of keeping them himself. Apparently, he just made them up to torture people. For that reason, I think it's fortunate that you seldom hear them today. Times have changed, and most adages seem obsolescent. For example:

"Fish and visitors stink after three days!" Franklin thought this one up—but it's scarcely valid these days. A refrigerator will keep the fish from going bad, and a can of deodorant placed in the visitors' bathroom will help them maintain a civilized odor.

"A penny saved is a penny earned." Won't do anymore, Ben! Today, a savings account pays less than one percent interest, but inflation is running at about five percent. So if you put your money in a savings account it will shrink up like a cheap bed sheet after it's been washed. Let's face it: "A penny saved is a penny lost."

"Little strokes fell great oaks." That won't work today either. If you want to "fell great oaks" ecologists will accuse you of endangering old growth forests, contributing to the greenhouse effect and causing acid rain. If, however, you're determined to "fell great oaks," why not use a chain saw?

"Children should be seen and not heard." I can still hear my grandmother quoting this one—but it would be hard to impose on kids these days. Today's kids chat endlessly on cell phones, play rap music on Walk Men and turn their car radios up to about ten on the Richter Scale. Change wording to: "Adults should be seen and not heard."

"If it relishes, it nourishes?" This old clunker is also a thing of the past. It meant that if something tasted good, (e.g., French fried potatoes, ice cream, T-Bone steak) it was good for you. These days, however, if food tastes good, you can be sure it contains too much sugar, saturated fat, carbohydrates or cholesterol. The modern version should read: "If it relishes—don't even think about it!"

"A man works from sun to sun, but a woman's work is never done." This rather chauvinistic adage may have been true in the days when the wife stayed home, minded the kids, cooked elaborate meals and cleaned the house. Today, however, the little woman probably punches a time clock, picks up the kids at day care center, serves a microwave dinner and then sprawls out on the couch watching television. Meanwhile, hubby does the dishes, bathes the kids, puts out the garbage, and cleans the house. Back to the old drawing board for this one!

"A rolling stone gathers no moss." When I was a kid this one puzzled me. I couldn't figure out why anyone would possibly want to gather moss. When I eventually came to understand that "moss" meant "money," the adage still puzzled me. What about Mick Jaggers and Keith Richards? They were apparently gathering plenty of moss.

Yep, old adages are a thing of the past—and I'm glad of it. They just served to make life miserable for people. If Franklin were around today he'd have to change most of them—starting with: "Fish *and adages* stink after three days!"

Common Cell Phone Types

I read recently that two billion people on planet earth own cell phones. Since the population of planet earth is about six billion, this means that every time you see any three individuals sky diving, walking tight ropes, robbing banks or climbing Mt. Everest, one of them is probably talking on a cell phone. This is one of the strangest phenomenons of our day, and we all need to understand it. Consequently, I have compiled the following list of "typical" cell phone users as an aid to readers. The material in this list is *not* based on a scientific poll and should be used only in case of emergencies.

1) The Zombie. Generally found in crowded malls, the Zombie is usually a teen-age girl who sports purple hair, thigh length shorts and metal ornaments in her navel. With a glassy look in her eyes, she walks straight ahead, talking on her cell phone while stepping on young children, elderly ladies and anybody too slow to get out of her way. Be careful—if awakened too quickly from her trance she may go ballistic.

2) The Phlumoxed Old Phone Phogy. This somewhat rare type—a Senior Citizen by trade—has just purchased a cell phone and doesn't know how to use it. He shakes the phone wildly, pushes buttons, flails his walking stick in the air, jumps up and down and yells, "By crackee—this thing ain't a-working." Do not attempt to help him—although he is old and feeble, rage and frustration make him dangerous.

3) The Phast Phlying Phone Phemme. This type (generally a curvaceous blonde) can be seen driving a lavender SUV down the street at 110 mph while filing her nails and cradling a cell phone under her neck. A dozen police cars follow her as she runs red lights and stop signs, leaving behind a trail of bewildered motorists. If you see one of these creatures, pull over to the side of the road, get out of your car—and pray!

4) The Phony Phinancial Phoner. This interesting type is often seen in restaurants, offices and public restrooms. Carefully dressed in suit, coat and tie, he juggles half a dozen cell phones into which he barks orders in a loud voice: "New York—buy ten thousand shares of Icarus Air Lines. Orlando—buy Disney World. Moscow—see if the Kremlin is for sale." Do not be fooled by this man. He is using dummy cell phones in an attempt to impress you. If ignored, he will burst into tears!

5) The Phrantic Phone Phighter. This pugnacious individual is fighting with his wife *via* cell phone. "What's that?" he yells. "You need a new washing machine because the old one leaks. Forget it. Buy a new mop. How's that? Your mother is flying in from Miami? I thought you said she had misplaced her broom." You will notice people gathering around and listening to the man. It's better than a soap opera!

6) The Check Out Chatterer. Often found standing ahead of you in line at the Supermarket, this maddening female is trying to corral several yelling brats while talking on a cell phone. "Hello, Matilda…This is Karen…Yes, I'm in line at the Super Market…Johnny, stop pulling on that lady's panty hose…I called to tell you about our trip to Canada…no, miss, it's Debit, not Credit…Reggie, stop going through that man's pockets…anyway, as soon as the plane landed in Quebec…Gloria, quit pouring Clorox on Mommy's shoes…"

As I said before, this list is intended to help you identify and understand typical cell phone users. Add to the list if you wish—I may have overlooked a few types.

978-0-595-39688-7
0-595-39688-7